D0505139

for 3 - 9s

Book 6

CHRISTIAN FOCUS PUBLICATIONS

We believe that the Bible is God's word to mankind, and that it contains everything we need to know in order to be reconciled with God and live in a way that is pleasing to him. Therefore, we believe it is vital to teach children accurately from the Bible, being careful to teach each passage's true meaning in an appropriate way for children, rather than selecting a 'children's message' from a Biblical passage.

© TnT Ministries
29 Buxton Gardens, Acton, London, W3 9LE
Tel: +44 (0)20 8992 0450

Published in 1998, reprinted 2001 by Christian Focus Publications Ltd.
Geanies House, Fearn, Tain, Ross-shire, IV20 1TW
Tel: (01862) 871 011 Fax: (01862) 871 699
www.christianfocus.com

Cover design by Douglas McConnach

Production by Shadbolt Associates. Tel +44 (0)20 8325 3131

This book and others in the series can be purchased from your local Christian bookshop. Alternatively you can contact TnT Ministries direct or place your order with the publisher.

Free license is given to copy visual aids and activities pages for use as class material only. We ask that each person teaching the material purchases their own copy. Unauthorised copying and distribution is prohibited.

TnT Ministries (which stands for Teaching and Training) was launched in February 1993 by Christians from a broad variety of denominational backgrounds who were concerned that teaching the Bible to children should be taken seriously. They have been in charge of the Sunday School of 50 teachers at St Helen's Bishopsgate, an evangelical church in the City of London, since 1984, during which time a range of Biblical teaching materials has been developed. TnT Ministries also runs training days for Sunday School teachers.

CONTENTS
On the Way for 3-9s / Book 6

Preparation of Bible material:
Thalia Blundell
David & Christine James

Editing:
David Jackman

Illustrations:
Ben Desmond

Craft Activities:
Andrew Blundell
Thalia Blundell
Sue Chapman
Julie Farrell
Annie Gemmill
Kathy Pierce
Sue Upcott
Nancy Olsen

On the Way works on a three year syllabus. It covers the main Bible stories from Genesis to the Acts of the Apostles. All the Bible stories are taught as truth and not myth.

Each year the birth of Jesus is taught at Christmas, and the death and resurrection of Jesus at Easter. Between Christmas and Easter the syllabus covers aspects of Jesus' life and teaching, and after Easter there is a short series on the Early Church. The rest of the year is spent looking at the Old Testament stories, covering broad sweeps of Old Testament history. In this way leaders and children gain an orderly and cohesive view of God's dealings with his people throughout the Old and New Testaments.

The lessons are grouped in series, each of which is introduced by a series overview stating the aims of the series, the lesson aim for each week and an appropriate memory verse.

Every lesson, in addition to a lesson aim, has Bible study notes to enable the teacher to understand the passage, suggestions for visual aids and an activity for the children to take home. One activity is suitable for 3-5 year olds, one for 5-7 year olds and one for 7-9s.

How to Prepare a Lesson

To prepare a Sunday School lesson properly takes at least one evening (2-3 hours). It is helpful to read the Bible passage several days before teaching it to allow time to mull over what it is saying.

When preparing a lesson the following steps should be taken -

1. PRAY!

In a busy world this is very easy to forget. We are unable to understand God's word without his help and we need to remind ourselves of that fact before we start.

2. READ THE BIBLE PASSAGE

This should be done **before** reading the lesson manual. Our resource is the Bible, not what someone says about it. The Bible study notes in the lesson manual are a commentary on the passage to help you understand it.

3. LOOK AT THE LESSON AIM

This should reflect the main teaching of the passage. Plan how that can be packaged appropriately for the age group you teach.

4. STORYTELLING

Decide how to tell the Bible story. Is it appropriate to recapitulate on what has happened in previous weeks? Will you involve the children in the presentation of the story? What sort of questions are appropriate to use? How will you ascertain what has been understood? Is there anything in the story that should be applied to their lives?

5. VISUAL AIDS

What type of visual aid will help bring the story alive for the children? Simple pictures may be appropriate. For stories with a lot of movement it may be better to use flannelgraphs or suedegraphs. In some instances models may be appropriate, e.g. the paralysed man being let down through a hole in the roof. Do remember that visual aids take time to make and this will need to be built into your lesson preparation.

6. CRAFT ACTIVITIES

Many of the craft activities require prior preparation by the teacher so do not leave it until the night before!

Benefits of On the Way

- Encourages the leaders to study the Bible for themselves.
- Chronological approach gives leaders and children a proper view of God's dealings with his people.
- Each lesson has 3 age related craft activities.
- Everything you need is in the one book, so there is no need to buy children's activity books.
- Undated materials allow you to use the lessons to fit your situation without wasting materials.
- Once you have the entire syllabus, there is no need to repurchase.

Teacher's Challenge

Located throughout this book are cartoons highlighting some aspects of the Bible passages. Hidden in one or more of these cartoons is a bookworm (see box on right - not actual size).

If you consider yourself observant and want a challenge, count the number of times the bookworm appears in this edition. The correct answer is on the back page. Don't look until you are sure you have found them all!

Samson

Overview

Week 1

THE STRONG MAN *Judges 13:1-10,24-25; 14:1 - 15:15*
To show how God chooses a deliverer for his people.

THE ENEMY DEFEATED *Judges 16:1-31*

Week 2
To show the consequences of sin, and God's power to restore those who are penitent.

Series Aims

1. To understand the stories in their context.

2. To understand the results of continued disobedience, and God's readiness to save if we turn to him in repentance and faith.

This series follows on from the lessons on Gideon (the last series in On The Way for 3-9s Book 5). The events studied also took place during the time of the Judges. The memory verse is the same as the one for the Gideon series.

Samson lived during the earlier part of the Philistine oppression, which extended into the days of the kings. The Philistines had settled on the coastal plain some years after the Israelites had conquered Canaan and, once established, they tried to expand into the Israelite hill country. They had the monopoly of smelting iron and this gave them a tremendous advantage, as the iron sword was far stronger than the bronze sword used by the Israelites. They worshipped a number of nature gods, amongst which was Dagon.

At the time of Samson, Israel had no strong national leadership and Philistine rule was not onerous. It was established by infiltration rather than force, and promised economic advantages to Israel. However, in those days nationality and religion went together - if the Philistines were the rulers it implied that Dagon was superior to Yahweh, (cf. Judges 16:23-24 1 Samuel 4:3-11; 5:1-6).

Samson was the son of Manoah, whose wife was barren. His birth was announced by the angel of the Lord (13:3) and he was to be a Nazirite from birth, i.e. consecrated for God's use. The Nazirite vow was normally only taken for a limited period (Numbers 6:1-21). Samson only took one of the stipulations seriously (long hair) - he was in contact with a corpse (14:8-9) and it is unlikely that he abstained from strong drink. If a Nazirite broke one of the 3 requirements his vow became violated and he had to be re-consecrated by sacrifice. This does not appear to have happened in Samson's case.

Samson's parents lived at Zorah, about 22 kms west of Jerusalem, on the borders of Dan and Judah, and he was from the tribe of Dan. He comes over in chapters 13-16 as being sensual, irresponsible, and with a lack of concern for the things of God - but God used him!

In these chapters in the book of Judges we see God, in his sovereignty, using Samson to highlight his people's plight under the Philistines. In the Scriptures we see that God can make use of a person, in spite of the quality of his life, e.g. Cyrus (Isaiah 44:28; 45:1-4), Nebuchadrezzar (Jeremiah 25:9; 27:6; 43:10), and Balaam (Numbers 22-24), but this must not be used by us as an excuse for sloppy living. We serve the God who commanded - 'you must be perfect - just as your Father in heaven is perfect!' (Matthew 5:48).

Memory Work

'Not by might nor by power, but by my Spirit,' says the Lord Almighty.

Zechariah 4:6

WEEK 1
The Strong Man

Preparation:
Read Judges 13:1-10,24-25; 14:1 - 15:15, using the Bible study notes to help you.

Lesson Aim:
To show how God chooses a deliverer for his people.

15:9   'Lehi' means jawbone.

15:15   The jawbone, complete with teeth, would have been a formidable weapon.

Lesson Plan

13:1   The pattern of events recorded in Judges 2:10-19 recurs again and again in the book of Judges.
1. a period of disobedience by the Israelites.
2. punishment through foreign oppression.
3. repentance.
4. raising up a judge as a deliverer.
5. this was often followed by a period of peace.
God punished his people in order to bring them to repentance.

13:4   Samson's mother also had to observe special requirements.

13:25   Samson's great power came from God, not from himself.

14:2   Marriage with a non-Israelite was warned against because of the risks of being led into idolatry (Deuteronomy 7:1-4).

14:5   Lions were not uncommon in Palestine in those days (cf. 1 Samuel 17:34-36, 1 Kings 13:23-32).

14:19   Ashkelon was an important Philistine city on the Mediterranean coast about 25 miles from Timnah.

This is the first of 2 lessons on Samson. Either show the children pictures of people doing jobs requiring specific tools, e.g. a man digging up the road, a doctor listening to a heart, a fireman using a water hose, etc. or mime various actions, e.g. digging, sweeping, dusting, etc. Each time ask the children what tool is being used. Could the job be done without the tool? In today's true story from the Bible we will find out about a man who had a special job to do. Ask the children to listen carefully so that at the end they can tell you the man's name, who gave him the job, what tool was given him to do the job (great strength).

At the beginning of the story for the older children remind them of the historical context - God's people are living in the land God has given them; Joshua has died; God's people have stopped following him so he has allowed the Philistines to rule over them. (See the series overview for information about the Philistines.) If you have used the lessons on Gideon from On The Way for 3-9s Book 5 remind the children about Gideon. At the end of the story go over the questions and teach the memory verse.

Visual Aids

Flannelgraph or pictures of Manoah, his wife, the angel (without wings - he looked like a man - 13:6,8), baby Samson, Samson as a man with long hair, Philistine girl, lion, donkey's jaw bone (see Visual Aids on pages 83-87. As this is quite a complex story to illustrate you might want to use the pictures from a Child's Story Bible.

It is important to explain the Nazirite vow to the older children before telling the story. Prepare a series of 5 strips of card with the following written on them: Nazirite, - no alcohol, - no grapes, raisins, - no cutting hair, - no dead bodies. Pin these up on a board as you explain what the Nazirite vow entailed. At the end of the story look at the statements to see which Samson kept.

Activities / 3 - 5s

Photocopy pages 8 and 9 for each child. Prior to the lesson cut along the dotted lines on both sides of Samson's hand on page 9. Cut out the shapes from the top of page 8 and place in an envelope for each child.

The children colour Samson and the shapes cut from page 8. Glue the robe, hair and beard onto Samson. Thread the jawbone through the slits either side of the hand and sellotape in place on the back of the picture.

Point out to the children that Samson's strength came from God. Just as they are gluing things onto Samson, God put his power into Samson - and what can be put in can also be withdrawn.

Activities / 5 - 7s

Each child requires pages 10 and 11 photocopied on card and yellow tissue paper to scrunch up as honey. (Play dough can be used instead of tissue paper.) Prior to the lesson cut out the shapes from page 10 and score and fold along dotted lines.

Instructions
- Colour the lion, fold along the dotted lines and glue the 2 sides of the beard together (see diagram).
- Fold the tail towards the feet and the fringe of the mane towards the nose.
- Colour the mane and glue to the top of the lion's head (see diagram).
- Glue the lion upside down onto page 11 where marked.
- Place scrunched up tissue paper or play dough in between the lions legs to represent the honey.

Activities / 7 - 9s

Photocopy pages 12 and the bottom part of page 8 for each child.

- Cut along the dotted lines on both sides of Samson's hand on page 12.
- Colour Samson and the symbols on the bottom of page 8.
- Cut out the symbols and glue in place on page 12. Glue the flame onto the chest (heart). Slot the jawbone through the slits either side of the hand and secure with sellotape on the back of the picture.
- Use the Bible passage to fill in the missing words on page 12.

Use the activity to point out to the children that Samson's great strength came from God and that God uses the people he chooses. Samson's life was not a godly one, but God still used him.

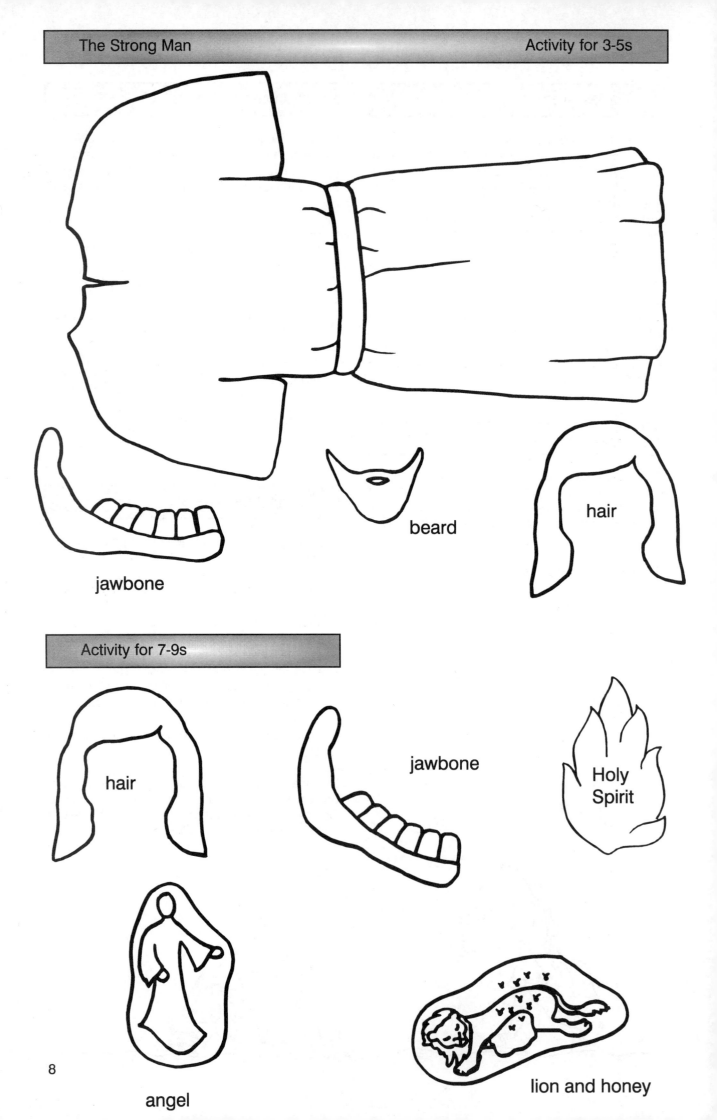

jawbone

beard

hair

hair

jawbone

Holy
Spirit

8

angel

lion and honey

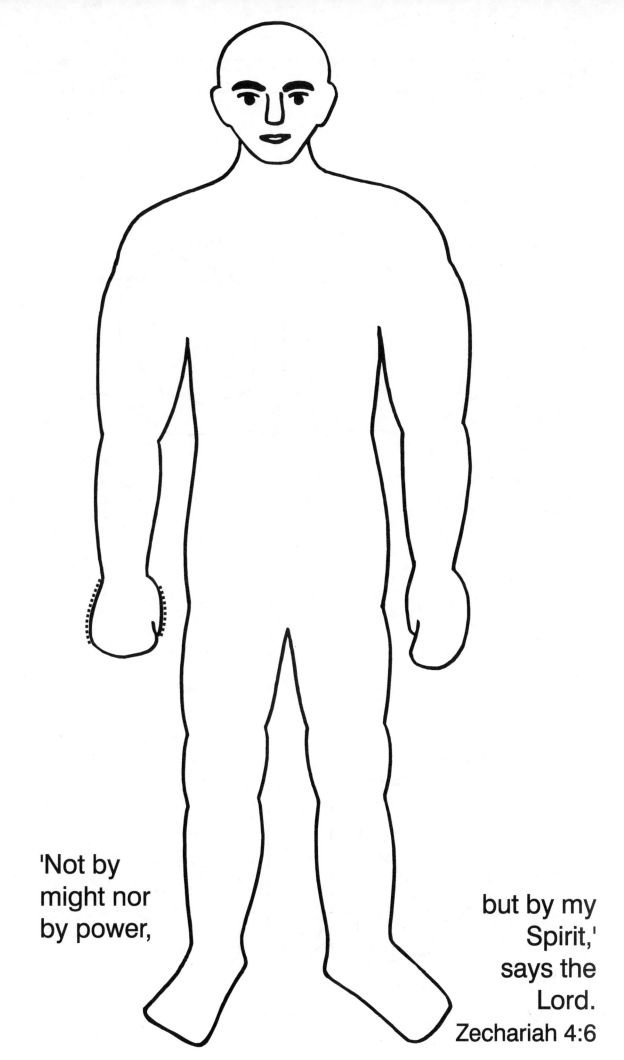

'Not by
might nor
by power,

but by my
Spirit,'
says the
Lord.
Zechariah 4:6

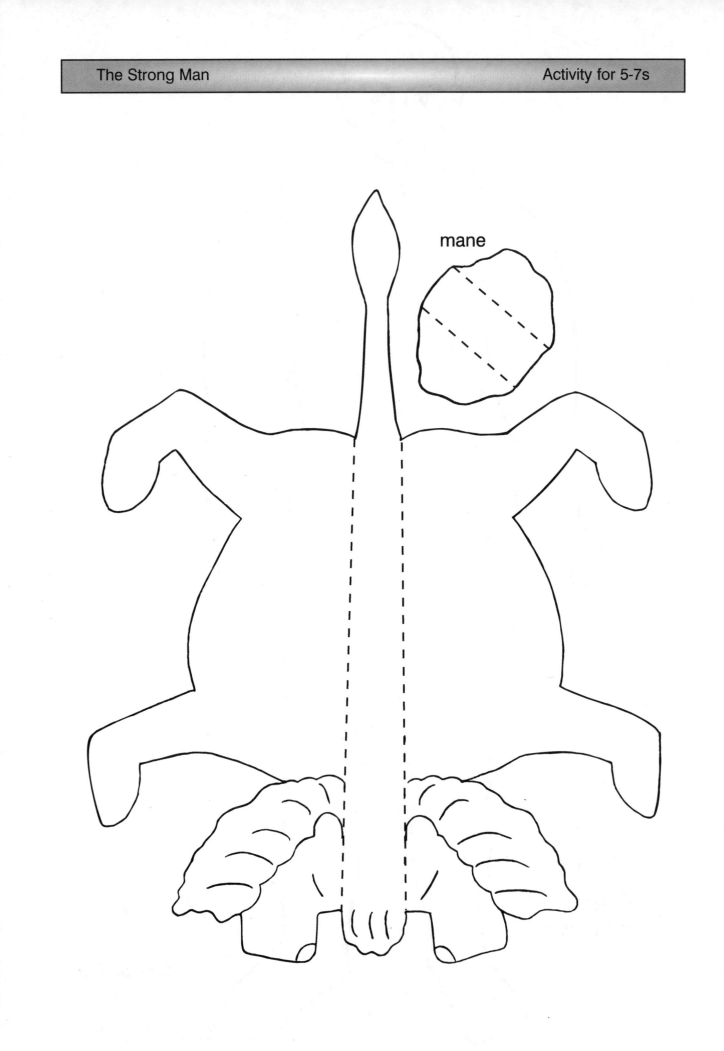

mane

Samson asked the Philistines the following riddle......

```
┌ ─ ─ ─ ─ ─ ┐
│           │
│           │
│           │
│           │
│ glue lion │
│   here    │
│           │
│           │
│           │
│           │
└ ─ ─ ─ ─ ─ ┘
```

'Out of the eater came something to eat;
Out of the strong came something sweet.'

'Not by might nor by power, but by my Spirit,' says the Lord Almighty.
Zechariah 4:6

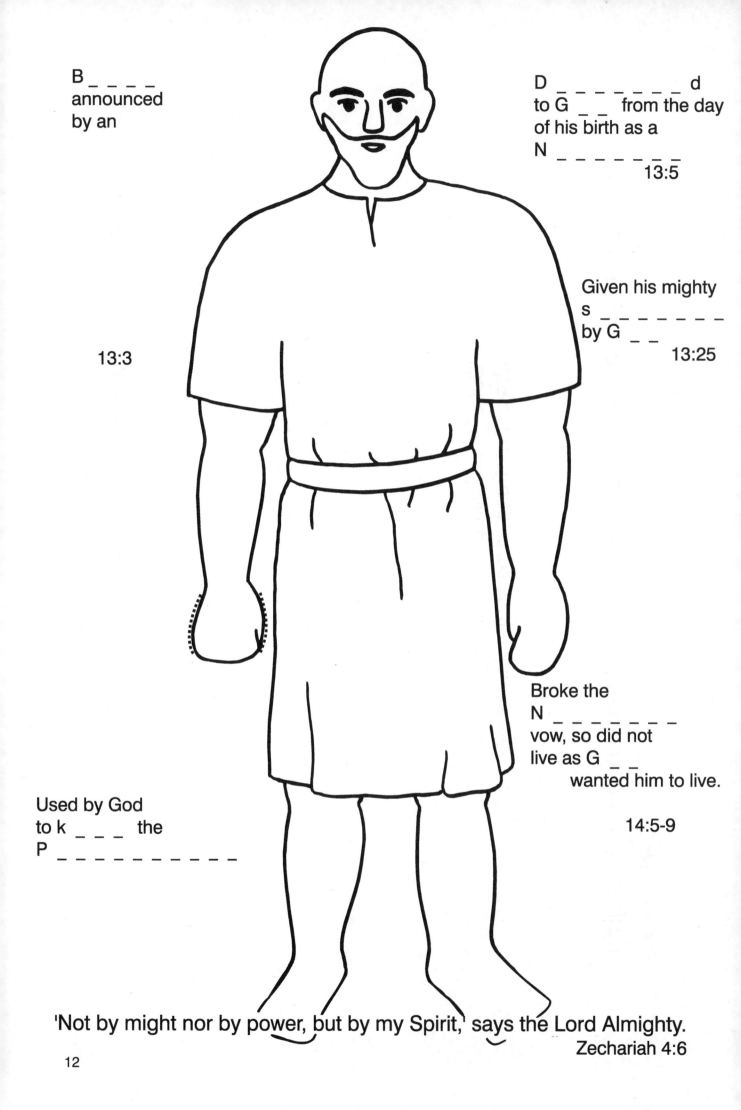

B _ _ _ _
announced
by an

13:3

D _ _ _ _ _ _ d
to G _ _ from the day
of his birth as a
N _ _ _ _ _ _ _
13:5

Given his mighty
s _ _ _ _ _ _ _ _
by G _ _
13:25

Broke the
N _ _ _ _ _ _ _
vow, so did not
live as G _ _
wanted him to live.

14:5-9

Used by God
to k _ _ _ the
P _ _ _ _ _ _ _ _ _ _ _

'Not by might nor by power, but by my Spirit,' says the Lord Almighty.
Zechariah 4:6

Preparation:
Read Judges 16:1-31, using the Bible study notes to help you.

Lesson Aim:
To show the consequences of sin, and God's power to restore those who are penitent.

Lesson Plan

16:1   Gaza was one of the 5 principal Philistine cities. It contained the chief temple to Dagon.

16:2   Maybe there was some convention that prohibited a man being killed in a house during the night - see also 1 Samuel 19:11.

16:3   Hebron is nearly 40 miles from Gaza. The hill was probably closer to Gaza and overlooked Hebron. It was an amazing feat of strength.

16:1-3   These verses demonstrate Samson's presumption and lack of watchfulness where sin is concerned. Both place and occupation were wrong - and his God-given strength was used to extricate himself from a position he should never have been in.

16:4   Delilah means worshipper.

16:5   1100 pieces of silver is a lot of money! The Philistine kings, unable to take Samson by force, used his infatuation with Delilah to trap him into revealing the secret of his strength.

16:6-14   Samson plays with fire -

16:15-21   - and gets badly burnt! Samson only had himself to blame.

16:20   **NB** He did not know that the Lord had left him.

16:21   Gouging out the eyes was a common and cruel treatment of enemies. Grinding was considered to be women's work (Exodus 11:5).

Start by recapping on last week's lesson, using a question and answer format, e.g. what was the name of the man in last week's story? What was special about him? (very strong), What did God tell Samson's mother he was never to do? (cut his hair). Remind the children that Samson's long hair was a sign that he was a special servant of God's (a Nazirite). The older children can be reminded of the other parts of the Nazirite vow and how Samson had broken them. In today's true story from the Bible we will find out whether Samson did what God told him. Ask the children to listen carefully so that they can tell you what happened to Samson and why. Tell the story.

At the end of the story go over the questions, bringing out the following points - Samson had his hair cut off and, as a result, lost his strength; this was because God had left him. This does not mean that people with long hair are strong. Point out that this is a very sad story. Samson had belonged to God from the time he was born, but as he grew older he stopped caring about God and what God wanted. Telling Delilah (one of God's people's enemies) about his hair not being cut off showed that he did not care about his relationship with God. The result was that God left him and he became the same as every other

13

man. God gave him back his strength when he turned to God for help. As a result Samson was able to do the job God had given him and destroy many Philistines. Revise the memory verse.

Visual Aids

Pictures
- Samson, a man with long (removable) hair. a cut out symbol of the Holy Spirit (flame, oil lamp, dove) to stick onto Samson. It can then be removed at the appropriate moment.
- Delilah
- money
- 7 bow strings
- ropes
- hair woven onto the loom
- scissors.

(See the activity pages 8, 15 and 16 and Visual Aids on pages 83-87.)
Remove the hair from Samson, then the Holy Spirit.
NB The removal of the hair denoted violation of consecration - there was nothing magic about the hair!!

Activities / 3 - 5s

Play matching pairs. Photocopy page 15 x 2 on card for each child and one set for each teacher and helper. (Ideally there should be one adult to every 4/5 children.) Prior to the lesson cut out each set of cards (9 pairs) and place in an envelope for each child. Colour the teacher's set.

Use the teacher's set to play the game. Jumble up the cards and place them face down on the table. The children take it in turns to turn over 2 cards. If the cards match the child takes the pair and has another turn. If the cards do not match they are replaced face down and the next child has a turn. The child with most pairs at the end of the game wins.

The children colour their own sets of cards if time permits.

Activities / 5 - 7s

Photocopy pages 16 and 17 for each child. Prior to the lesson cut out the pictures and arrow from page 16 and place in an envelope for each child. The children colour the pictures and glue them in the appropriate place on page 17. Fold the arrow in half along the dotted line and glue to give extra rigidity. Colour the arrow and attach it to page 17 at X using a split pin paper fastener. Move the arrow to point to each picture in turn asking, 'Did Samson lose his mighty strength because .... ?' Make sure the children realise there was nothing magic about Samson's hair - it was only a symbol of his relationship with God. There was no strength in the hair!

Activities / 7 - 9s

Photocopy pages 18 and 19 back to back and the pictures on page 16 for each child. Cut out the pictures from page 16. Work through pages 18 and 19 as a group, filling in the gaps and gluing the pictures in the appropriate places. Colour the pictures if time permits.

Make sure the children realise there was nothing magic about Samson's hair - it was only a symbol of his relationship with God. There was no strength in the hair!

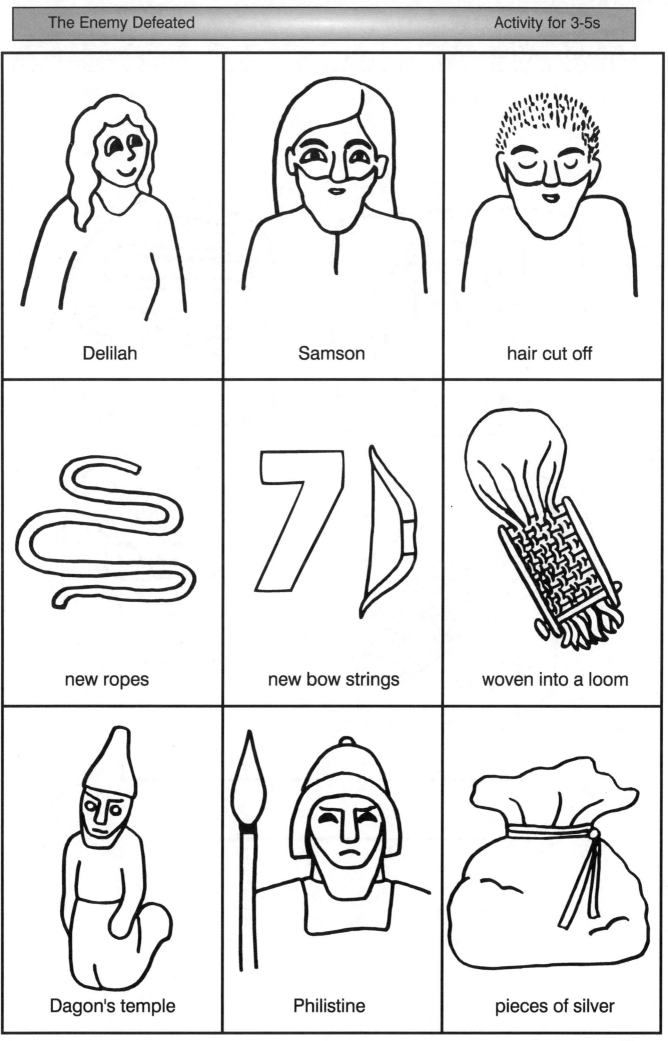

Delilah

Samson

hair cut off

new ropes

new bow strings

woven into a loom

Dagon's temple

Philistine

pieces of silver

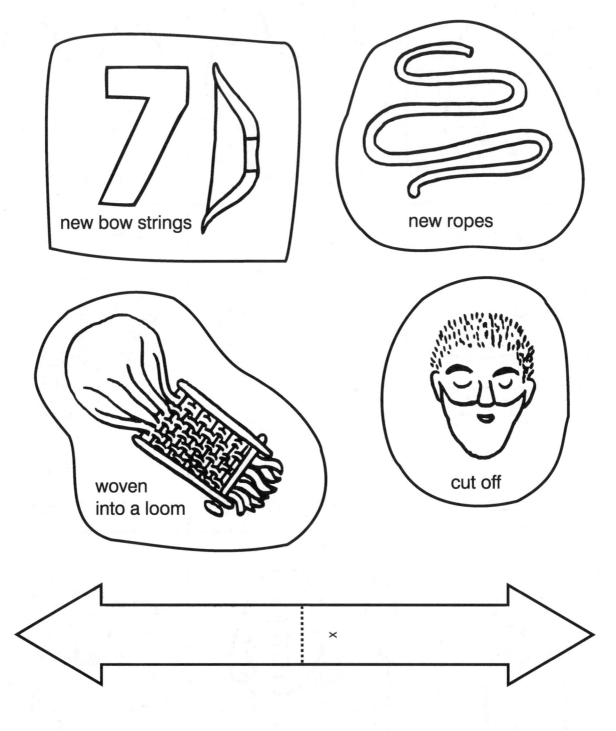

new bow strings

new ropes

woven into a loom

cut off

Samson lost his mighty strength because ....

he was tied up with

his hair was

x

his hair was

he was tied up with

his hair was

which showed he was no longer set apart for God - and God's Spirit left him.
'Not by might nor by power, but by my Spirit,' says the Lord Almighty.
Zechariah 4:6

17

The Bible story comes from Judges 16:1-31

Samson was a N _ _ _ _ _ _ _   - he was set apart for God
(Judges 13:5). God had said that Samson's hair must never be
 c _ _ . Samson was very s _ _ _ _ _   because God's
S _ _ _ _ _   was with him (Judges 13:25).

Samson was very silly - he fell in love with D _ _ _ _ _ _ _ ,
who was an enemy (Judges 16:4). Delilah asked Samson to tell
her why he was so s _ _ _ _ _   (Judges 16:6).

Samson told Delilah a lie -
if she tied him up with

he would lose his strength.
Delilah did so -
        it did not work.

Samson told Delilah another
lie - if she tied him up with

he would lose his strength.
Delilah did so -
        it did not work.

Samson told Delilah a
third lie - if his hair was

he would lose his strength.
Delilah did so - it did not work.

18

Then Samson told Delilah
the truth - if his hair was

he would lose his strength.
Delilah did so -
        and it worked.

When Samson's hair was cut
he was no longer a N _ _ _ _ _ _ _ ,
his relationship with G _ _   was b _ _ _ _ _ .
God's S _ _ _ _ _   left Samson (Judges 16:20), but he did
 not know it - he thought he was still as s _ _ _ _ _   as ever.

The P _ _ _ _ _ _ _ _ _ _ _   captured Samson and made
him their slave (Judges 16:21).
Samson's hair started to grow again (Judges 16:22).

One day the Philistines had a great feast to offer sacrifice to their
god, D _ _ _ _   (Judges 16:23). They sent for Samson to
e _ _ _ _ _ _ _ _ _   them (Judges 16:24-25).

Samson stood between the 2 p _ _ _ _ _ _   that held up the
building (Judges 16:26). The building was c _ _ _ _ _ _ _
with people (Judges 16:27).
Samson asked G _ _   to help him (Judges 16:28) - and God
did so. God gave Samson back his s _ _ _ _ _ _ _   (16:28),
and Samson pushed against the p _ _ _ _ _ _   (16:29) and
the building fell down, killing every one inside.

Ruth

Overview

Week 3

RUTH AND NAOMI   *Ruth 1:1-22*
To teach how Ruth came to trust God.

Week 4

RUTH AND BOAZ   *Ruth 2:1 - 4:22*
To show that God takes care of those who trust him.

Series Aims

1. To understand the story in its context.

2. To learn that God takes care of those who trust him.

The book of Ruth is set in the last years of the Judges (Ruth 1:1; 4:13-17), a time when chaos reigned and 'everyone did just as he pleased' (Judges 21:25). It is a story about a Moabite girl, a foreigner, who turned to Israel's God and became part of his people, and in doing so was blessed. Her son became the grandfather of Israel's great king, David.

Book outline

Chapter 1   A Jew named Elimelech, his wife Naomi and their 2 sons, Mahlon and Chilion, leave the Promised Land because of famine and go to Moab to live. There Elimelech dies, the 2 sons marry Moabite women, and 10 years later both sons die. Naomi hears that food is now plentiful in Canaan and determines to return. She urges her daughters-in-law to stay in Moab; Orpah decides to, but Ruth insists on accompanying Naomi. Together they travel to Bethlehem, Naomi's home town.

Chapter 2   Ruth goes to collect grain for food (Leviticus 19:9-10, Deuteronomy 24:19) and works in Boaz's field (Boaz is a close relative of Naomi's).

Boaz, having heard of Ruth's goodness to Naomi, orders her to work only in his field and offers her food and water. Ruth goes home that night with food for Naomi and discovers that Boaz is a kinsman.

Chapter 3   Naomi uses Jewish law to provide a husband for Ruth (Leviticus 25:25, Deuteronomy 25:5-10). Ruth places herself under the protection of Boaz. Boaz offers to be her kinsman-redeemer - but first of all the one who is a closer relative must be given the opportunity to fulfil the law.

Chapter 4   Boaz, in the presence of witnesses, asks the close relative to fulfil the law by buying the field and marrying Ruth. The close relative refuses, so Boaz marries Ruth. They have a son, Obed, who becomes the grandfather of David.

The theme of the book is redemption. Boaz foreshadows Christ - he comes from Bethlehem, he is able to redeem, he is not under obligation to redeem, he decides to redeem by grace, and the redemption is costly. Ruth foreshadows us - a total outsider (pagan, a widow, a woman), but brought into the centre of God's plan.

In telling this story to the children we need to emphasise how God looked after Ruth and blessed her (Ruth 2:20).

Memory Work

Trust in God, and he will help you.

Psalm 37:5

20

WEEK 3
Ruth and Naomi

Preparation:	Lesson Aim:
Read Ruth 1:1-22, using the Bible study notes to help you.	To teach how Ruth came to trust God.

Lesson Plan

1:1-2   The story takes place during the time of the Judges. It was a time when many Jews turned their back on God.
Elimelech means 'God is King'.
Naomi means 'pleasant'.
Mahlon means 'weakling'.
Chilion means 'pining'.
Moab was a fruitful land east of the Dead Sea, about 50 miles from Bethlehem. (For the origin of Moab see Genesis 19:30-38). The Moabites were idolaters and were often at war with Israel.
Bethlehem means 'house of bread'.

1:11   It was customary for a childless widow to be married to her late husband's younger brother (Deuteronomy 25:5-10).

1:16-17   Similar to to-day's marriage vows! Note that Ruth's declaration had nothing to do with whether circumstances were beneficial or not. Ruth had come to trust God, Orpah had not.

1:20   Marah means 'bitter'.

1:22   Barley harvest began in April and was followed by wheat harvest.

These 2 lessons on Ruth deal with the concept of trust. Make a list of 8-10 people, some of whom the children will trust, e.g. parents, Sunday school teacher, school teacher, doctor, dustman, stranger. Ask the children to separate the people into 2 groups - those they trust and those they do not. Discuss why they trust some people and not others. How do they know they really trust someone? (By doing what they say even when they do not understand why.) In today's true story from the Bible we will learn about a family. Some of them trusted God and some did not. Ask the children to listen carefully so that they can tell you the name of the person who did not trust God and the person who did. (Elimelech did not trust God - when circumstances were adverse he left the land God had given his people and went to the land of God's enemies. Ruth trusted God.)

At the end of the story go over the questions, then teach the memory verse. Next week we will find out if Ruth was right to trust God.

Visual Aids

Pictures or flannelgraph. You will need figures of the 6 characters, 2 sets of houses (1 for Bethlehem and 1 for Moab), and a long road in between. If using pictures, cover the road with transparent PVC adhesive. Bluetak can be stuck on the back of the figures and they can then be moved along the road as the story progresses (NB Naomi must be double sided). For the 3 women photocopy page 23. For the 3 men see the visual aids section on pages 83-87.

Activities / 3 - 5s

Photocopy pages 23 and 24 for each child. Prior to the lesson cut out the 3 figures from page 23 and place in an envelope for each child. The children colour the figures and the background. Ask the children who each figure represents. (Naomi is the older lady, Ruth is going in the same direction as Naomi and Orpah is returning home to Moab.) Glue the figures onto page 24 to complete the picture.

Activities / 5 - 7s

Each child requires 3 wooden clothes pegs, 3 rubber bands, 3 different coloured squares of material 11 x 11 cm and a block of oasis approximately 15 x 8 cm. (Oasis can be purchased from a florist.)

Instructions
- Draw a face on each peg (see diagram). Orpah looks sad, Naomi and Ruth look happy.

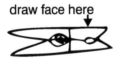
draw face here

- Fold the squares of material into triangles and make up the peg figures (see diagram).

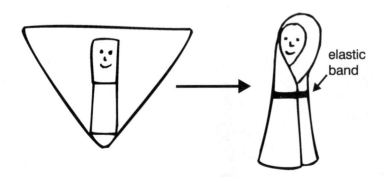
elastic band

- Stick the peg figures into the block of oasis with Ruth and Naomi facing one way and Orpah facing the other.

Activities / 7 - 9s

The activity consists of 2 parts. Each child requires page 25 photocopied on paper and page 26 photocopied on card, a yoghurt pot filled with damp soil or sand, a lollipop stick (or similar) and a sticky label on which is written, 'rooted in the one, true, living God'.

Page 25 is a picture of Ruth's family tree, showing her relationship to David and Jesus. Do this as a class activity, filling in the gaps. Cut out Ruth's tree from page 26. Look up the Bible verses in the apples and write in each apple what Ruth had to give up when she went with Naomi (parents, gods, country). Point out to the children that God does not ask everyone to give up these things when they trust in him, but he does require us to put him first. Fill in the blanks on Ruth's speech bubble. Sellotape the stick to the back of the tree, with the end of the stick protruding a few centimetres from the bottom. Plant the tree in the yoghurt pot and stick the label around the pot. Discuss what it means to be rooted in the one, true, living God.

Orpah

Ruth

Naomi

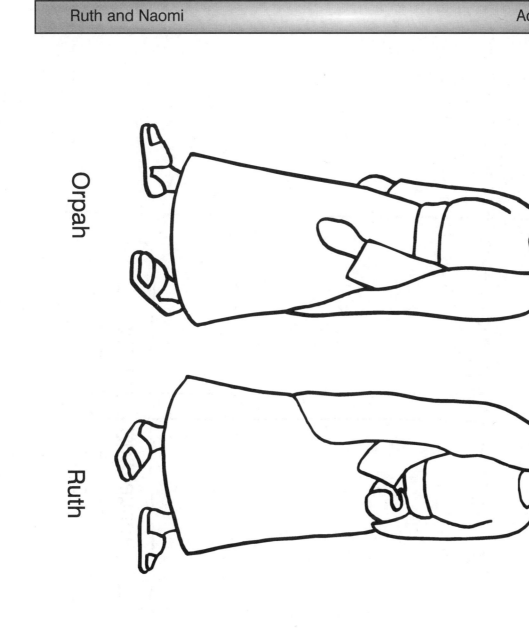
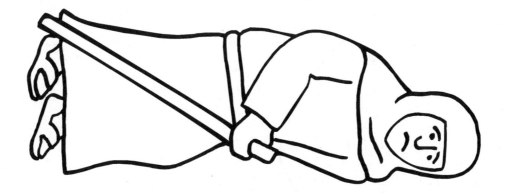

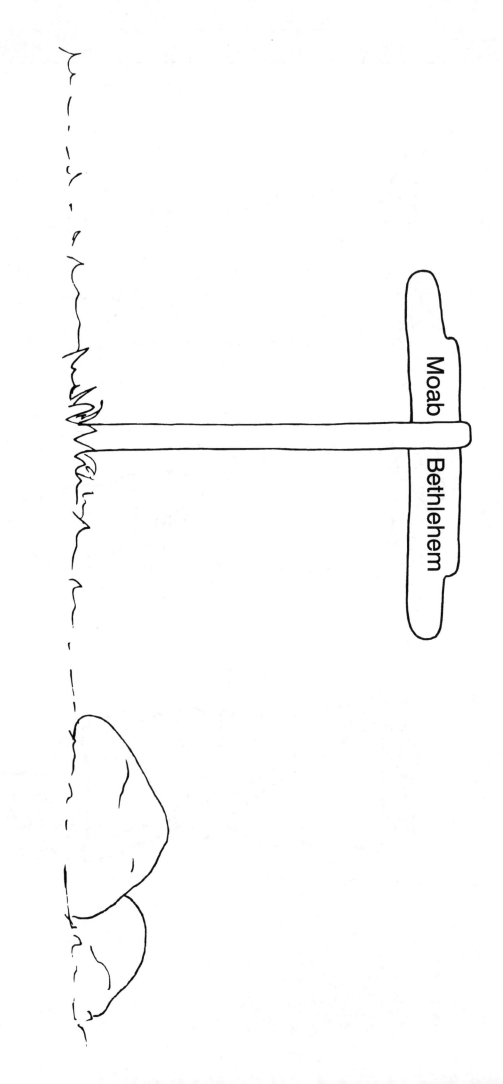

Trust in God, and he will help you.   Psalm 37:5

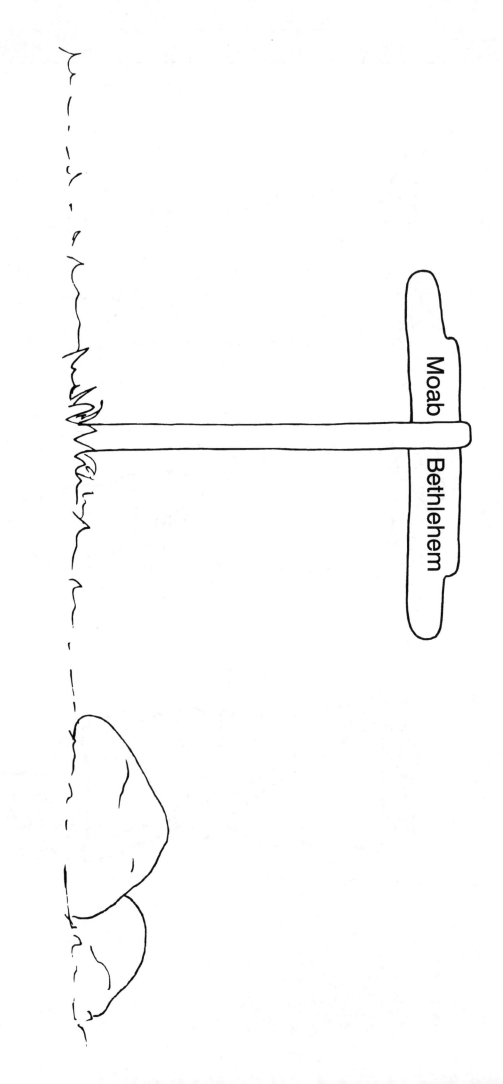

Trust in God, and he will help you.   Psalm 37:5

Ruth's Family Tree

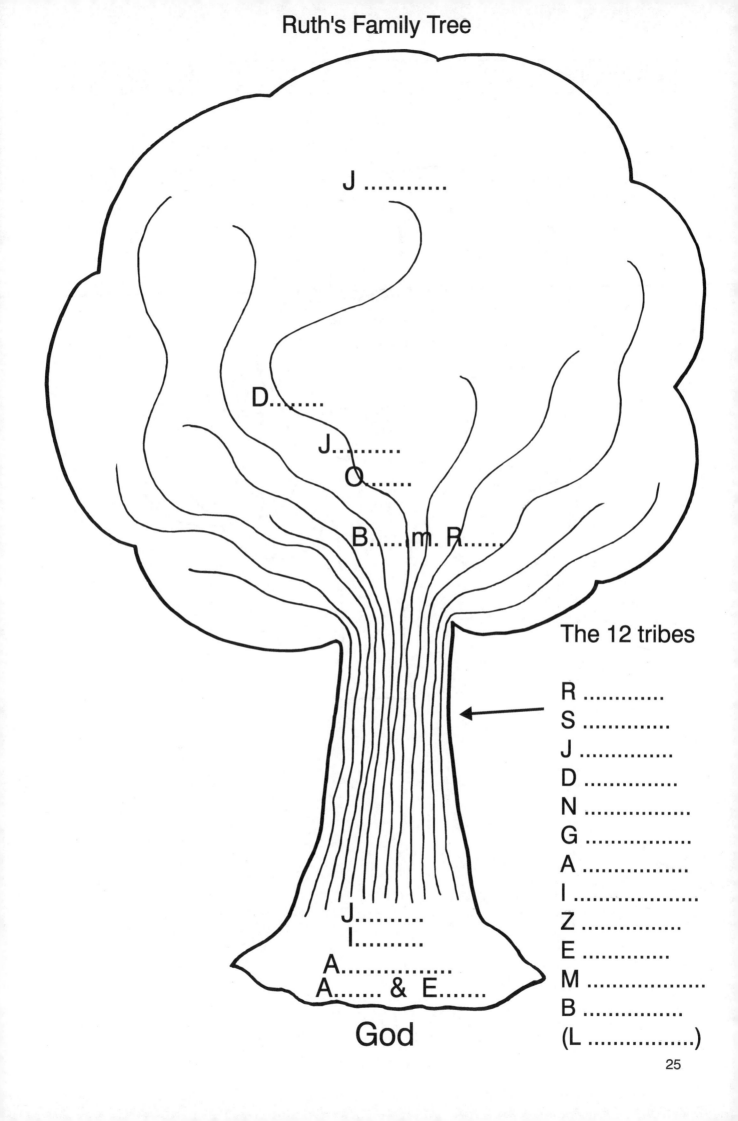

J ....

D.........

J...........

O.......

B........m. R........

J...........

I.........

A................

A........ & E.......

God

The 12 tribes

R ....

S ....

J ....

D ....

N ....

G ....

A ....

I ....

Z ....

E ....

M ....

B ....

(L ....)

25

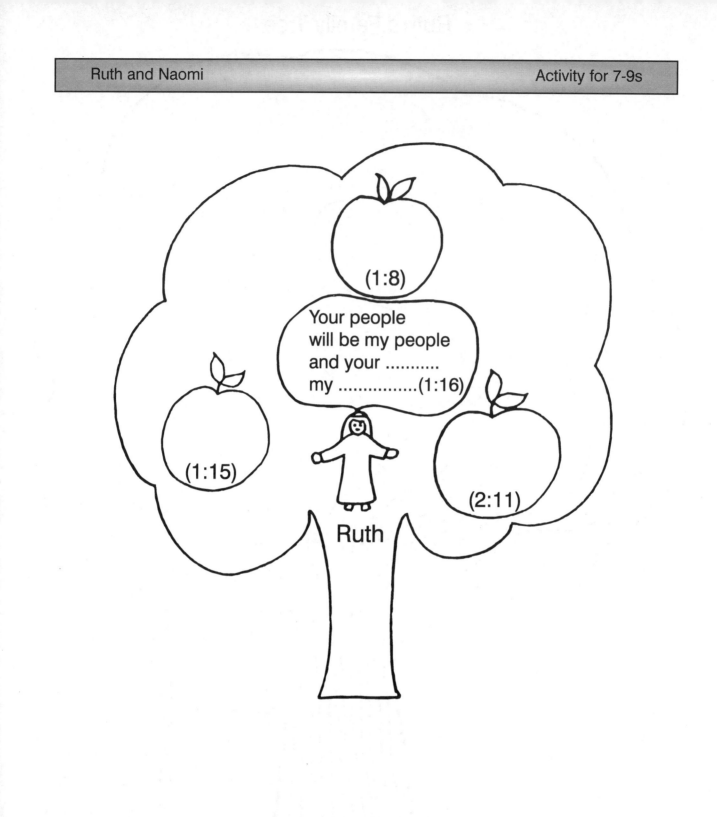

Preparation:
Read Ruth 2:1 - 4:22, using the Bible study notes to help you.

Lesson Aim:
To show that God takes care of those who trust him.

2:2   See Leviticus 19:9-10, Deuteronomy 24:19.

2:3   'It so happened' - an example of God's providence.

2:4   Israelites were very careful not to take God's name in vain (Commandment 3) so this greeting denoted that Boaz was a God-fearer.

2:17   A lot of corn from gleaning! (Gleaning involved picking up the remnants of grain left by the harvesters).

2:20   The Hebrew word translated 'close relative' means kinsman-redeemer (see Leviticus 25:23-28, Deuteronomy 25:5-10). The closest relative was legally responsible for buying back the field. He also had the opportunity to marry the widow (as was customary), although only the brother-in-law was obliged to marry the widow.

3:1-4   This seems very forward to us, but Naomi had the sanction of the law behind her.

3:7   The men took it in turns to guard the harvest at night.

3:9   'Spreading a cloak over' symbolised marriage (cf. Ezekiel 16:8).

3:12-13   Boaz was legally obliged to put Ruth's case to her closest relative before he could take responsibility for her himself.

3:22   The large amount of barley was a tangible assurance to Naomi of Boaz's good will.

4:1   The city gate was the place where business was transacted and disputes heard. See also 2 Samuel 15:1-2.

4:5-6   Elimelech had the right to have an heir to inherit his field. By taking Ruth to wife and raising a son for Elimelech, the kinsman-redeemer lost part of his sons' inheritance because they would not inherit what he had bought, and any other sons born to the marriage would share the kinsman-redeemer's property along with his previous sons.

4:7   Handing over the sandal was a symbolic ceremony to show that the right of possession had passed from one person to another (cf. Joshua 1:3).

4:12   The story of Judah and Tamar (Genesis 38:1-30), although unsavoury, referred to Levirate marriage (Deuteronomy 25:5-10). Tamar had been tacitly refused, but Boaz had honoured his obligation. Perez, who was born to Tamar as a result of her trick, was an ancestor of Boaz, so there was local interest in the story.

Lesson Plan

Remind the children of the last lesson. Ruth had learnt to trust God. How do we know? (She left everything and went with Naomi to the land God had given to his people.) Ask the children if they trust God to look after them. What sort of things does God do to show that he cares for them? You might like to enlarge the pictures on page 29 to use with the younger children. In today's true story from the Bible we will find out how God looked after Ruth. Ask the children to tell you at the end how God did this. Tell the story.

At the end of the story go over the questions. Revise the memory verse.

Visual Aids

Pictures of the main characters (see pages 23 and 31). Point to them as you tell the story.

Activities / 3 - 5s

Photocopy page 29 on paper and page 30 on card for each child. Prior to the lesson cut out the cube from page 30, score and fold along dotted lines and glue together with the flaps on the inside. Cut out the pictures and place in an envelope for each child.

Discuss with the children how God helped Ruth by supplying her needs. Ask them what sort of things God gives them, e.g. food, home, family, toys, friends. Ask them to pick the appropriate picture for each thing. The children colour the pictures and glue them onto the cube.

Activities / 5 - 7s

Photocopy page 31 for each child. Go through each of the questions with the children until they reach the end of the maze. Then go over the right path with them a second time and mark it with a coloured pen. Colour Ruth and Boaz and fill in the missing word of the memory verse.

Activities / 7 - 9s

Each child makes a woven heart with the story of Ruth on one side and the memory verse on the other. For each child photocopy pages 32 and 33 back to back on paper, page 34 on coloured card and page 35 on a different coloured paper.

Preparation
- Cut up the lines on page 33 from the bottom to the line underneath 'The Story of Ruth'. Stick the bottom of the page below the dotted line back together again with sellotape.
- Cut out the heart shape from page 34 leaving the frame intact.
- Cut page 35 into horizontal strips and discard the top and bottom strips. Clip the strips together with a paper clip for each child.

Instructions
- Weave the strips in and out of page 33 so that the finished story makes sense. Then draw in relevant pictures where there are blanks.
- Turn the page over and fill in the missing letters of the memory verse.
- Glue the card frame over page 32.

This activity is based on the idea that Ruth's life (and ours) is like a tapestry. God knows the finished picture and will give Ruth all the help she needs if she trusts him. But Ruth does not see the finished picture, so her life (and ours) may look a bit confused and uncertain at times, just like the underside of a tapestry.

Trust in God,
and he will
help you.
Psalm 37:5

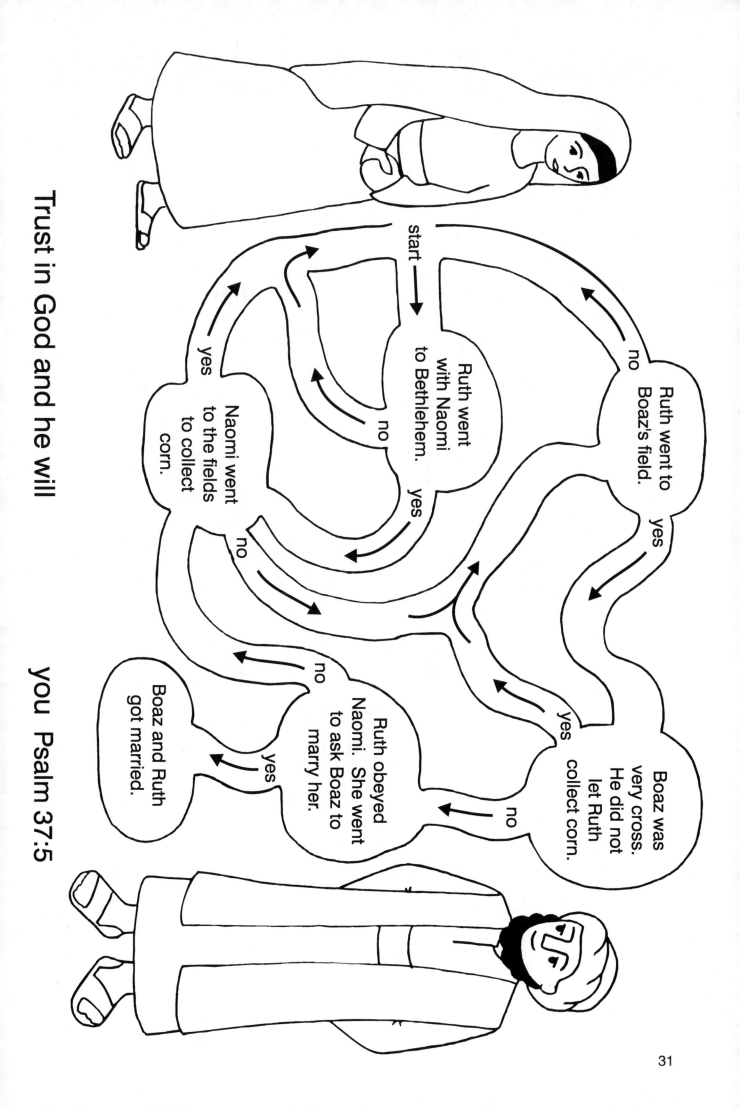

Trust in God and he will

you Psalm 37:5

31

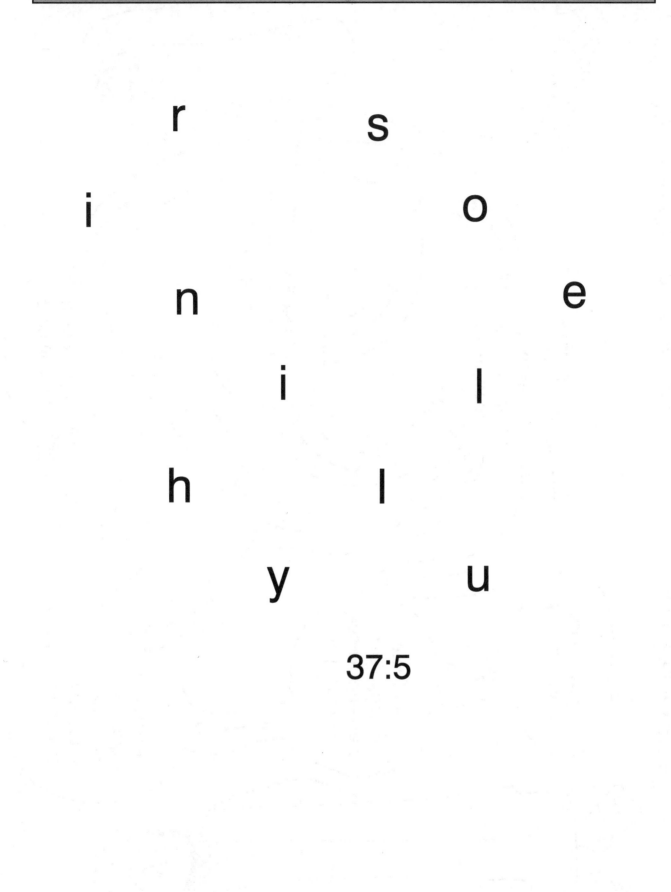

r   s

i   o

n   e

i   l

h   l

y   u

37:5

The Story of Ruth

10 years later

Back they both went to Bethlehem.

went to Moab for food.

but Ruth insisted on going with her.

Ruth discovered Boaz was a relative of Naomi.

Naomi decided to return to

Boaz's field.

The closer relative refused.

Their sons, Mahion and Chilion,

.....and your God my God' (1:16)

Ruth claimed Boaz's protection.

'Praise be to the Lord!' (4:14)

She urged her daughters-in-law to stay in Moab.

and he gave her food and water.

They had a son, Obed.

but he said the closer relative must have first chance.

cut   cut   cut   cut   cut   cut   cut

God takes care of those who trust him.

cut
out

Elimelech and Naomi, (who were Jewish),	Elimelech died.	married Ruth and Orpah.	
	both sons died.	Bethlehem.	
Orpah stayed,	She said, 'Your people will be my people....		
	Ruth collected grain in	Boaz told her to only work in his field	He said to Ruth, 'May you be richly rewarded by God ....
.......under whose wings you've taken refuge.' (2:12)	Naomi used Jewish law to provide a husband for Ruth.		Boaz offered to be her kinsman-redeemer,
	He must not only buy the field - he also had to marry Ruth!	So Boaz married Ruth.	
	Obed was the grandfather of King David. .		

Samuel

Week 5

A PRECIOUS BABY   *1 Samuel 1:1-28; 2:11,18-21*
To teach that God answers the prayers of those who trust him.

Week 6

AN OBEDIENT BOY   *1 Samuel 3:1-21*
To teach the need to listen to God's word and do what he says.

Series Aims

1. To understand the stories in their context.

2. To teach the need to trust and obey God.

Samuel was the last of the Judges (Acts 13:20) and the first of the Prophets (Acts 3:24). He came from the tribe of Ephraim but was of Levitical stock (1 Chronicles 6:33-38). His parents were Elkanah and Hannah, who had previously been barren and had dedicated Samuel to God before he was born. After Samuel was weaned he was brought up by Eli the priest at the temple of Shiloh.

Samuel experienced God's call whilst still a boy and when he was adult became both priest and prophet (1 Samuel 3:19-21; 7:9). He was also a judge (1 Samuel 7:15-16) and appointed his sons as judges

(1 Samuel 8:1-2). However, his sons were not godly men, so the tribal leaders came to Samuel to ask for a king. God told Samuel to accede to this request (1 Samuel 8:7). Samuel then met with Saul and, on God's orders, anointed him as king of Israel. After Saul had been rejected by God Samuel anointed David privately to be king after Saul. He eventually died of old age at Ramah, where he had lived (1 Samuel 7:17; 25:1).

This series looks at Samuel's birth and early life and we need to impress on the children the importance of responding to God from an early age.

The memory verse is the same as the one for the previous series on Ruth.

Memory Work

Trust in God, and he will help you.

Psalm 37:5

WEEK 5
A Precious Baby

Preparation:
Read 1 Samuel 1:1-28; 2:11,18-21, using the Bible study notes to help you.

Lesson Aim:
To teach that God answers the prayers of those who trust him.

1:2   Polygamy was not God's original plan for mankind (Genesis 2:21-24), but was allowed for under the Law of Moses (Deuteronomy 21:15-17). The instances recorded in the OT, e.g. Abraham, Jacob, David, Solomon, show that the practice led to family problems. Barrenness was considered to be a calamity. Children were a sign of God's blessing (Psalm 127:3-5).

1:3   Joshua set up the Tabernacle at Shiloh (Joshua 18:1), which became the centre of worship. (The temple had not yet been built.)

1:4   The meat was part of the sacrificial meal (Deuteronomy 12:4-7) and everyone received a share. Hannah was only entitled to one share, because she only had herself to feed.

1:11   Hannah's words were part of the Nazirite vow (Numbers 6:1-5).

1:12-13   It was normal practice to pray aloud.

1:21   The yearly sacrifice was probably the Passover sacrifice.

1:22   It was only obligatory for the men to attend the Passover feast.

1:24   We do not know how old Samuel was. Probably 3 bulls - 1 for a burnt offering, 1 for a sin offering and 1 for a peace offering. The flour and wine were also for the offerings (see Numbers 15:8-10).

2:18   Probably a simple loin cloth. Samuel's duties would have included learning, reading, studying the Law, prayers and practical duties such as lighting lamps, running errands, etc.

Lesson Plan

Start by asking the children how many different ways they could let someone know they had a need. (You might need to specify the person and the need.) List them on the board. For younger children you could use pictures, e.g. 2 people talking together, a telephone, a letter, semaphore flags, etc. Ask the children how they know the message has been heard. In today's true story from the Bible we will hear about a lady who wanted something very badly. Ask the children to tell you at the end the name of the lady, what she wanted, who she asked for it and how she knew her request had been heard. Tell the story.

At the end of the story go over the questions and revise the memory verse. (The memory verse for this series is the same as for the previous one.) Talk about the different answers God gives. We know that God hears us when we pray, but he does not always answer, 'Yes'; sometimes the answer is, 'No', other times it is, 'Wait'.

Visual Aids

Yoghurt pot people and a 'temple' made from a cardboard box with pillars made from paper towel centres.

Requirements for people
Yoghurt pots or plastic drinking cups, egg cartons, scraps of material, wool, rubber bands, cotton wool, sellotape, glue, pens.

Instructions
Cut the head from an egg carton and sellotape onto a yoghurt pot or plastic cup. Draw on a face. Dress with a piece of material secured round the middle with wool or a rubber band. Tuck the bottom edge of the material inside the bottom of the pot. Attach the head-dress in similar fashion to the robe. The

women's head-dresses are wrapped around and secured with a stitch at the front. Glue on cotton wool as a beard for Eli and Elkanah.

The altar is made from a small box (matchbox) covered with gold paper.

The candlestick is cut out of gold card (see diagram). Glue a toothpick to the back of the upright with the point protruding from the base. The candlestick can be stuck into a blob of bluetak to make it stand up.

Leave the aids for use next week.

Activities / 3 - 5s

Photocopy page 40 on card for each child.

Preparation
- Cut the page in half along the cutting line.
- Fold Hannah in half along the dotted line and cut her out complete with tabs. Using a sharp pair of scissors or cráft knife, cut along the dotted lines around the inner edge of Hannah's arms and the outer edge of one of them.
- Cut out the baby and fold in half along the dotted line.
- From the remaining section cut off the part containing the cradle, leaving a square piece of card to be a base for the model.
- Cut out the cradle. Cut along the solid lines. Score and fold along the dotted lines.

Instructions
- Colour the cradle and glue it together.
- Colour Hannah and the baby Samuel.
- Press in the fold on the baby to give him some shape.
- Fold back the tabs on the sides and bottom of Hannah. Glue the tabs together so that she will stand up (see diagram).
- Glue Hannah onto the base facing towards the memory verse. Glue the cradle in front of her. Tear up a paper tissue to make fluffy bedding in the cradle. Either lay baby Samuel in the cradle or slot him into Hannah's arms with his head to the left as you look at the model.

Make one in advance to show the children.

38

Activities / 5 - 7s

The children make a booklet to illustrate the story. Each child requires one sheet of coloured and one sheet of white paper. Fold the 2 sheets of paper in half with the coloured paper on the outside and staple in the middle to form a booklet. Number the white pages 1 to 4. Write on the pages as follows:

Front cover   *Samuel, a Precious Baby*
Page 1   *Hannah was very sad. She did not have any children.*
Page 2   *Hannah prayed to God.*
Page 3   *God heard Hannah's prayer. She had a baby son. She named him Samuel.*
Page 4   *When Samuel was old enough Hannah took him to live with Eli. Samuel served God all his life.*
Back cover   *Trust in God, and he will help you. Psalm 37:5*

The children draw and colour pictures to illustrate the words on each page.

Activities / 7 - 9s

Photocopy pages 41, 42 or 43 depending on the Bible version your children use. Having answered all the questions on the page (including revision of the memory verse), discuss the importance of keeping promises with the children. Discuss how knowing God will help them to trust him for their daily needs.

Samuel, a Precious Baby
1 Samuel 1:1-28; 2:11, 18-21

Trust in God, and he will help you.
Psalm 37:5

cut

cut

cradle

tab

fold line

tab

fold line

tab

tab

tab

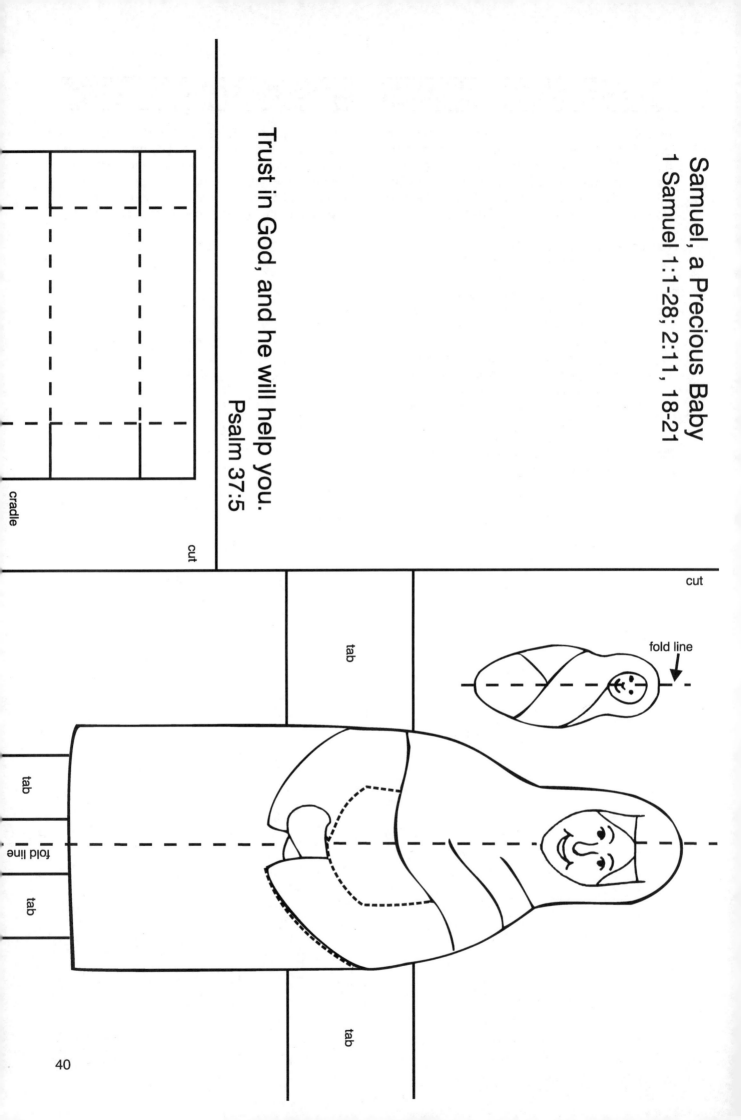

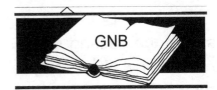

What did Hannah learn? Using your Bible to help you, answer the questions from the passage and place your answers in the grid below. The story is found in the book of 1 Samuel. The numbers in brackets tell you what chapter and verse to look up.

1. Which tribe did Elkanah come from? (1:1)

2. What did Peninnah have that Hannah did not? (1:2)

3. Where did the family go each year to worship God? (1:3)

4. What did Peninnah do to Hannah? (1:6)

5. What did Hannah do as she prayed? (1:10)

6. What did Hannah ask God for? (1:11)

7. What did God do to Hannah's prayer? (1:19)

8. What did Samuel do for God? (2:11)

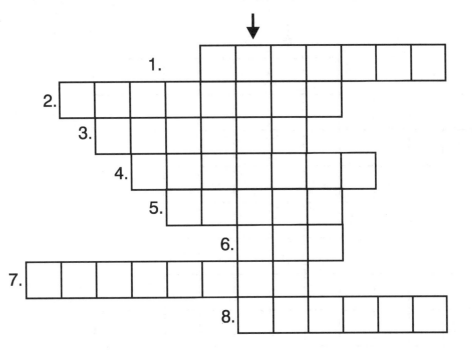

Now write the letters in the column indicated by the arrow into the spaces below.

God always keeps his   _ _ _ _ _ _ _ _ .

Which promise have we learnt during this series?

.... Psalm 37:5

DISCUSS

How did God do this for Hannah?
What promise did Hannah make to God?
Did Hannah keep her promise?

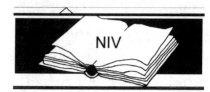

What did Hannah learn? Using your Bible to help you, answer the questions from the passage and place your answers in the grid below. The story is found in the book of 1 Samuel. The numbers in brackets tell you what chapter and verse to look up.

1.   Which tribe did Elkanah come from? (1:1)
2.   What did Peninnah have that Hannah did not? (1:2)
3.   Where did the family go each year to worship God? (1:3)
4.   In which building was Eli sitting? (1:9)
5.   What did Hannah ask God to look upon? (1:11)
6.   What did Hannah ask God to give her? (1:11)
7.   What did God do for Hannah? (1:19)
8.   What did Samuel do for God? (2:11)

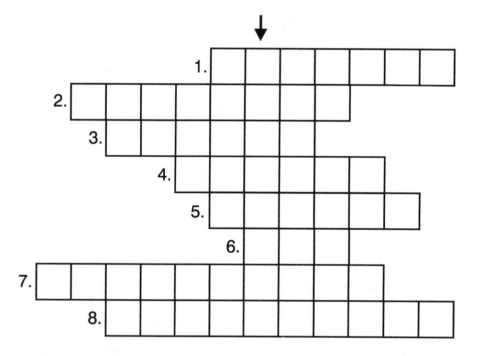

Now write the letters in the column indicated by the arrow into the spaces below.

        God always keeps his   _ _ _ _ _ _ _ _ _ .

Which promise have we learnt during this series?

.... Psalm 37:5

How did God do this for Hannah?
What promise did Hannah make to God?
Did Hannah keep her promise?

What did Hannah learn? Using your Bible to help you, answer the questions from the passage and place your answers in the grid below. The story is found in the book of 1 Samuel. The numbers in brackets tell you what chapter and verse to look up.

1.   Elkanah was an .... (1:1)

2.   What did Peninnah have that Hannah did not? (1:2)

3.   Where did the family go each year to worship God? (1:3)

4.   In which building was Eli sitting? (1:9)

5.   What did Hannah ask God to look upon? (1:11)

6.   What did Hannah pour out before the Lord? (1:15)

7.   What did God do for Hannah? (1:19)

8.   What did Samuel do for God? (2:11)

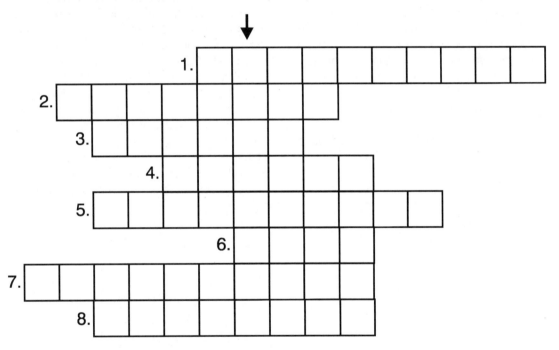

Now write the letters in the column indicated by the arrow into the spaces below.

God always keeps his _ _ _ _ _ _ _ _ _ .

Which promise have we learnt during this series?

.... Psalm 37:5

How did God do this for Hannah?
What promise did Hannah make to God?
Did Hannah keep her promise?

Lesson Aim:
To teach the need to listen to God's word and do what he says.

Lesson Plan

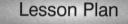

3:3	The sanctuary was split into 2 parts, separated by a curtain. The Ark of the Covenant was in the inner section. As only the High Priest could enter this section once a year on the Day of Atonement, Samuel must have been sleeping in the outer section. The lamp stand was the only means of light (see Exodus 25:31-40; 27:20-21).
3:13	See 1 Samuel 2:12-17,22-34.
3:18	Note Eli's acceptance of God's righteous judgment (cf. Genesis 18:25).

Start with a listening game like Simon Says. Children who get the instructions wrong miss a turn. At the end ask the children if it was important for them to listen to you. What happened if they didn't do what you said? Remind the children of last week's story, using a question and answer format. Did God listen to Hannah? Do we want God to listen to us? Should we listen to God? In today's true story from the Bible we will find out what Samuel did when God spoke to him. Ask the children to listen carefully so that they can tell you what God said to Samuel and what Samuel did about it. Tell the story.

At the end of the story go over the questions and revise the memory verse. Point out to the children that Samuel not only listened to God, but also did what God said.

Visual Aids

See instructions for week 5. Add in a yoghurt pot person for Samuel as a boy. You also need 2 beds and covers - 1 for Eli and 1 for Samuel. The beds can be made from the lid of a margarine container covered by a scrap of material.

Activities / 3 - 5s

Photocopy page 46 on white paper and page 47 on dark blue paper for each child. Prior to the lesson cut around 3 sides of the flap on page 47, leaving the dotted line intact. Cut out Samuel, the candlestick and the square with words on and place in an envelope for each child.

Instructions
- Colour Samuel and the candlestick, flames and light.
- Glue Samuel and the candlestick onto page 47 with Samuel below the flap.
- Put glue around the edges of the square with words and attach it to the back of page 47 so that the words are visible when the flap is lifted. Lift the flap to show God calling to Samuel.

Activities / 5 - 7s

Photocopy pages 48 and 49 for each child. Prior to the lesson cut out the hatched areas from page 49.

Instructions
- Colour Samuel and the picture.
- Cut out the wheel and attach it to the back of the picture using a split pin paper fastener through the dots. Cut out the tab and glue it to the wheel so that it can be moved round easily.
- Cut out Samuel and fix to the picture at X using a split pin paper fastener.
- Start with Samuel lying down and turn the wheel until his name appears in the upper window. Then sit Samuel up and turn the wheel until his answer appears in the lower window.

NB Samuel, the wheel and the tab may need to be cut out for younger children.

Activities / 7 - 9s

Each pair of children need a photocopy of page 51, a counter to be their 'car' and a pencil to trace their route. The teacher needs the instructions on page 50.

This activity is designed to teach the children the importance of listening carefully and following instructions. The teacher gives the children instructions for finding their way through the maze to each word of the Bible verse. If the children follow the instructions correctly they will end up with the words of the verse in the right order. At the end they should look up the reference to check they are correct. Some routes commence at 'start', others carry on from the word already found.

At the beginning explain to the children that they are going on a car journey. Each car contains a driver and a navigator. The activity sheet is a map, so will have to be turned around as they go in order to get their left and right instructions correct. Ensure that the children understand what is 'left', 'right', a crossroads, a junction, a T-junction and an exit. Top and bottom exits refer to the exit nearest the top or bottom of the maze as labelled.

At the end of the exercise discuss with the children how they listen to God and the importance of obeying his word.

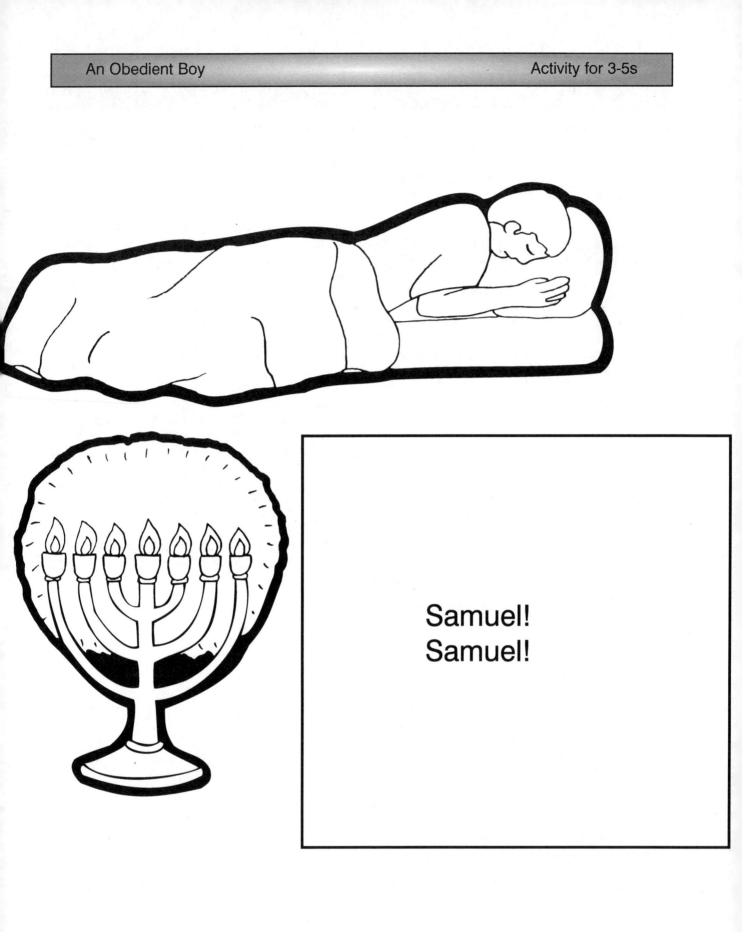

Samuel!
Samuel!

Samuel, an Obedient Boy   1 Samuel 3:1-21

Trust in God, and he will help you.   Psalm 37:5

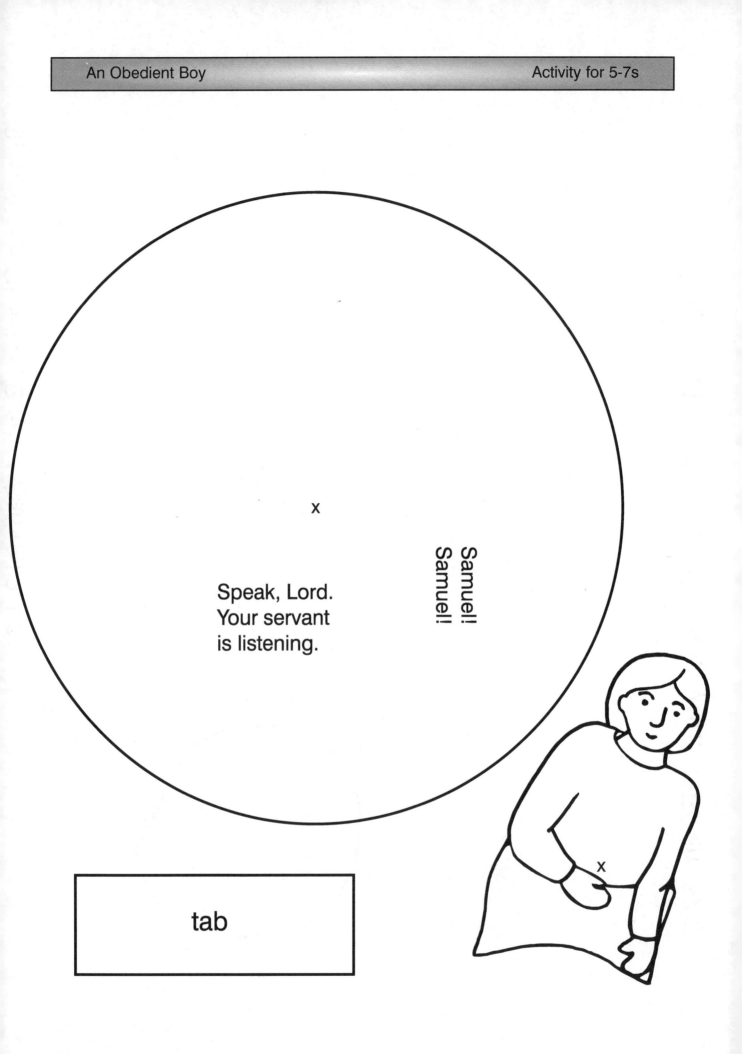

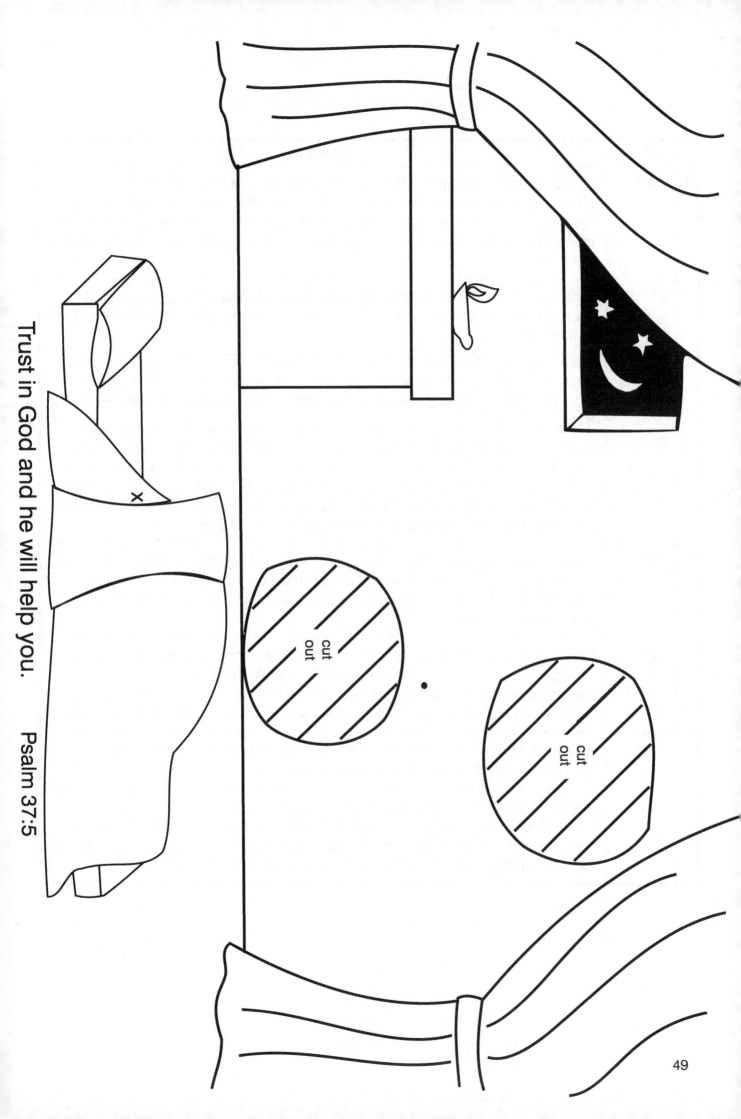

Trust in God and he will help you.   Psalm 37:5

cut out

cut out

49

Instructions for Car Treasure Hunt

	Start	Route
1	start	Leave by the middle exit. Go to the cross-roads and keep straight on. Go straight over the next cross-roads. At the next cross-roads turn right, then take the first left. Go to the next cross-roads and turn left. Go straight over the next cross-roads then take the second road to the right. Write the word at the foot of the page.
2	where you finished	Leave by the middle exit, pass a road on your left and go to the T-junction. Turn left and go straight on until you come to a word. Write the word at the foot of the page.
3	start	Leave by the bottom exit, pass a road on your right and go to the T-junction. Turn right and go to the next cross-roads. Turn left and then take the next left turn. Go straight on until you come to a word. Write the word at the foot of the page.
4	start	Leave by the middle exit. At the first junction turn right. Pass a road on your right then go over 3 cross-roads. At the fourth cross-roads turn left. Take the next left turn and go to the T-junction. Turn right then take the next left. Go straight over the next 3 junctions and come to a T-junction. Turn left, then right, and go straight to the word. Write it at the foot of the page.
5	start	Leave by the middle exit and go straight on to the second junction. Turn right, go straight over 2 cross-roads and pass a road on your left. Come to a T-junction and turn left. Go straight on until you get to a word. Write the word at the foot of the page.
6	where you finished	Leave by the top exit, pass a road on your left and one on your right. At the next junction turn left. Take the next right turn. At the next junction turn left. Go straight over the next cross-roads and pass a road on your left. Turn right at the next junction and go straight to the word. Write it at the foot of the page.
7	start	Leave by the top exit and pass a road on your left. At the next junction turn left. Go straight over the next cross-roads. At the next cross-roads turn right. Go straight over 2 cross-roads. At the third cross-roads turn left. Go straight over the next cross-roads. At the next junction turn left, then turn left again. Take the next road on your right and go straight over the next cross-roads. At the next junction turn right. Go straight over the next cross-roads. At the T-junction turn right and go straight to the word. Write it at the foot of the page.

In order to discover the verse you must listen carefully and follow the instructions you are given. When you have finished, look up the reference at the foot of the page to check you have got it right.

top

bottom

1 Samuel 3:9

Saul

Overview

Series Aims

1. To understand the stories in their context.

2. To understand that God calls us to obey him, and persistent disobedience has consequences.

Saul was the son of Kish, of the tribe of Benjamin (1 Samuel 9:2). He was a good looking young man, a head taller than others, courageous (1 Samuel 11) and merciful (1 Samuel 10:27; 11:12-13). He was chosen by God to be Israel's first king.

At this time the Israelites were suffering under the lordship of the Philistines. (The Philistines, having control of iron smelting, were able to make stronger weapons than other nations.) The people wanted a warrior-king to help them, thus rejecting the spiritual kingship of God. God warned them through Samuel of the problems they would encounter it they had a king (1 Samuel 8), but the people persisted in their request and God granted it.

The first lesson deals with the Israelites asking for a king and Samuel's meeting with Saul, the one chosen by God to be king. The second lesson picks up the story with Saul's anointing, prior to his return home. On his way home everything Samuel told him would

happen comes to pass and God gives him a new heart. The lesson ends with Saul being crowned king.

In the third lesson we see Saul disobeying Samuel's instructions and offering the sacrifice to God. (Samuel was recognised as God's mouthpiece, 1 Samuel 3:19-20.) As a result God denies him a dynasty. This lack of trust on Saul's part is contrasted with Jonathan's trust in God's help in his battle against the Philistines. The fourth lesson deals with Saul disobeying God's clear instructions to destroy the Amalekites and all their animals. When Samuel faces Saul with his disobedience he makes excuses for his behaviour and God rejects him as king.

The story of Saul is a tragic one of a man chosen by God who is finally rejected by God because of his persistent disobedience.

In this series we are building on the previous two series. Ruth demonstrated God's care of those who trust him; Samuel showed the importance of trusting and obeying God; Saul shows what happens when we repeatedly disobey.

Memory Work

If you love me you will obey my commandments.

John 14:15

WEEK 7
Searches for Donkeys

Preparation:
Read 1 Samuel 8:1 - 9:26, using the Bible study notes to help you.

Lesson Aim:
To teach that God wants us to serve and obey him.

8:2   Beersheba lies at the southern extremity of Israel, perhaps indicating the extent of Samuel's influence.

8:4   The Israelites wanted the political and military security of a king, fearing what would happen after Samuel died. The behaviour of his corrupt sons (Samuel's appointment, not God's) was probably the last straw. They remembered how they had suffered previously at the hands of the Philistines when they had no one to lead them. A king would be a visible figure-head who would make them feel secure. In much the same way they had previously worshipped the idols of Baal and Astarte (1 Samuel 7:4). Therefore, just as they preferred to put their trust in the gods of their neighbours rather than the true saviour God, so they preferred a king along the pattern of their neighbours, rejecting God as their king. They failed to recognise that they had been defeated, not because they had no king, but because of their sin. Instead of learning from these past errors and turning to God in repentance to trust and serve him, they wanted to by-pass him and defeat the enemy in their own way (see Judges 8:22-23).

8:9   The monarchy seems to have been permitted rather than appointed. What was wrong about the request was the attitude of the elders who made it. God is responding not to the elders but to the suffering of his people under the Philistines. Monarchy was a concession to man's weakness, which in God's grace and mercy became part of his plan for man's ultimate salvation in the person of Jesus the king.

9:1-25   Saul is pictured here as a young innocent abroad, obedient to his father, an impressive young man who showed a willingness to seek the Lord. He would have known of Samuel, (Judge of Israel), but probably had not met him before.

9:4-5   Saul travelled from Gibeah in Benjamin, his home town (10:10-11,14), through the hill country to Shalisha. From there he came back down to Benjamin, probably travelling through Benjamin from east to west, and back up to Samuel's home town, Ramah (7:17; 9:18). Ramah was in the district of Zuph.

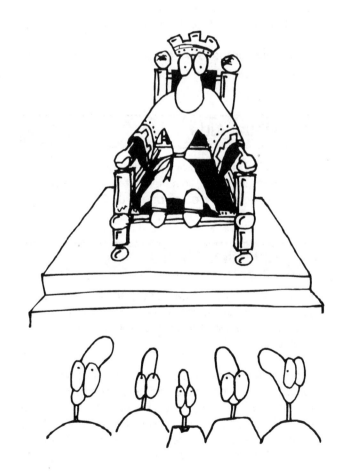

Lesson Plan

For the younger children prepare one donkey each (see visual aids on pages 83-87), label them with the child's name and hide them in the class area. Once all the donkeys have been found and given to their owners tell the children that today's true story from the Bible is about someone who was looking for lost donkeys. Ask them to tell you at the end his name and who he met whilst he was looking for the donkeys.

For the older children start by asking them which brand of trainers, jeans, sweat tops they wear. Why do they choose those brands? (Children are very keen to wear the well known brands and be like the 'cool' people.) In today's true story from the Bible we will learn about some people who wanted to be like every other nation. Ask them to listen carefully so that they can tell you who wanted to be like every other nation, In what way, and who was chosen.

As this series starts with Samuel as an old man you need to remind the children of the previous lessons on Samuel. Point out that many years have passed and Samuel is now very old. Tell the story.

At the end of the story go over the questions and teach the memory verse.

Visual Aids

Flannelgraph or pictures of individual figures. You need Samuel, Saul, his servant and a crowd of people (see visual aids on pages 83-87).

Activities / 3 - 5s

Make cone figures of Saul and Samuel. Photocopy page 55 on card for each child. Prior to the lesson cut out all the pieces and place in an envelope for each child.

The children colour the pieces, then the bodies are folded into a cone shape and glued or stapled down the back. Place the head on the body by slotting the long tab through the hole at the top of the cone. Glue or staple the base of the tab inside the front of the body. Glue on Samuel's priestly turban.

Activities / 5 - 7s

Make a crown. Each child requires page 56 photocopied on paper and an A4 sheet of coloured card. Prior to the lesson cut out the 8 'jewels' and the jigsaw pieces of the Bible verse and place in an envelope for each child. Cut out the 2 halves of the crown from the sheet of card (see diagram). Cut off the 2 black triangles and discard.

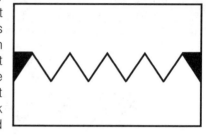

Staple the 2 halves together at one end. The children glue on the 'jewels', representing the things that would have to be given to the king (see diagram). Assemble the memory verse along the bottom edge 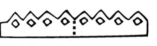 and glue in place. The 'jewels' can be coloured if time permits. Fit the crown onto the child's head and staple/sellotape the 2 ends together.

Activities / 7 - 9s

Photocopy page 57 on coloured card for every 4 children and page 58 on paper for each child. Cut out a crown for each child and punch a hole through the 2 outside circles. Attach a length of wool to the crown, making a loop big enough to go over the child's head (see diagram).

Go through page 58 as a class activity. Give each child a crown. Ask them if God is their king. Those whose answer is 'yes' should write 'God is my King' on their crown. Tell them to wear the crown round their neck under their clothes to remind them that even though their king is not visible he is greater than any human king.

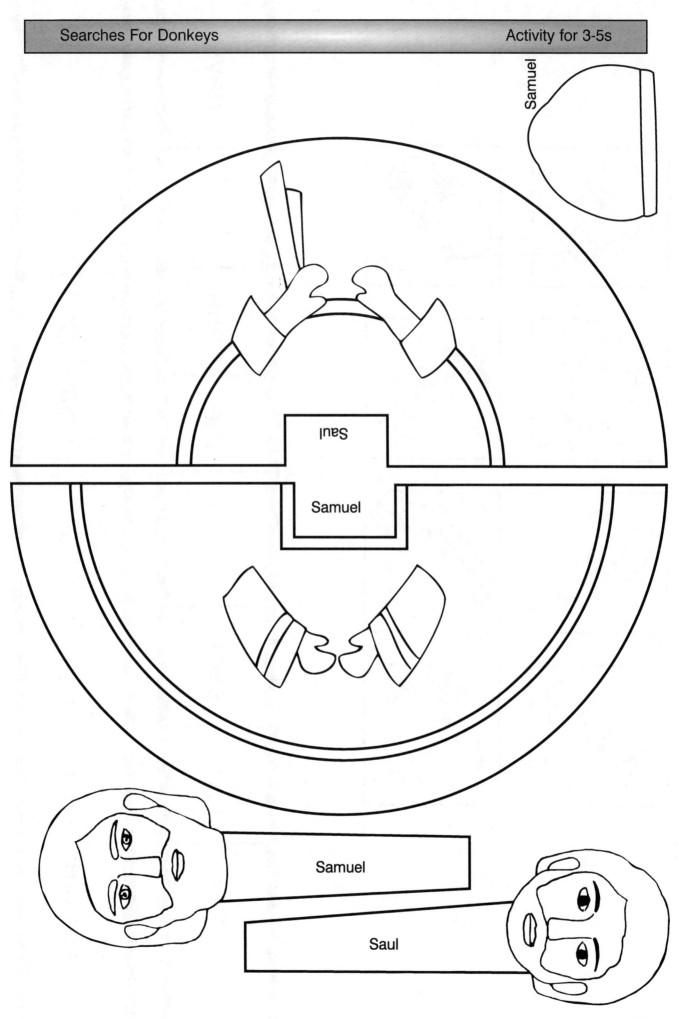

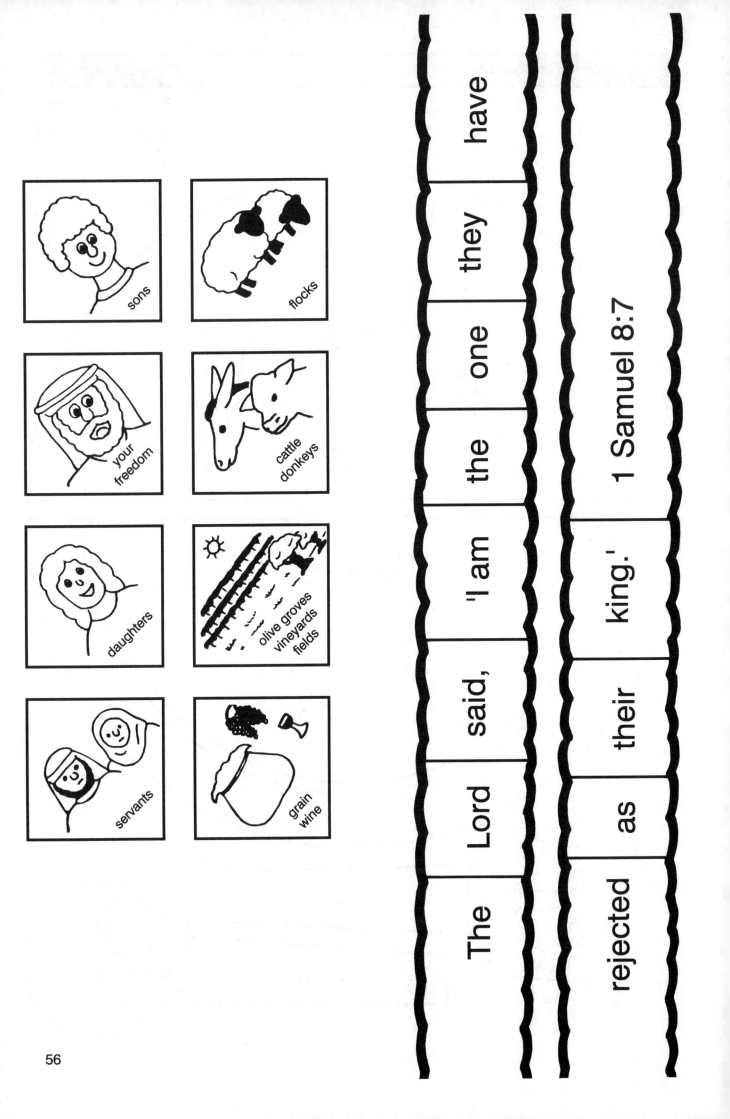

sons

flocks

your freedom

cattle donkeys

daughters

olive groves vineyards fields

servants

grain wine

The Lord said, 'I am the one they have rejected as their king.'

1 Samuel 8:7

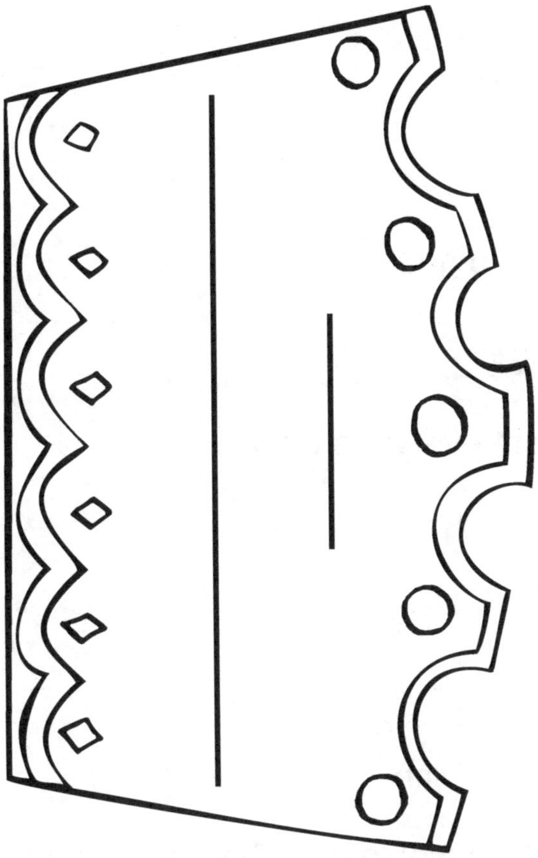

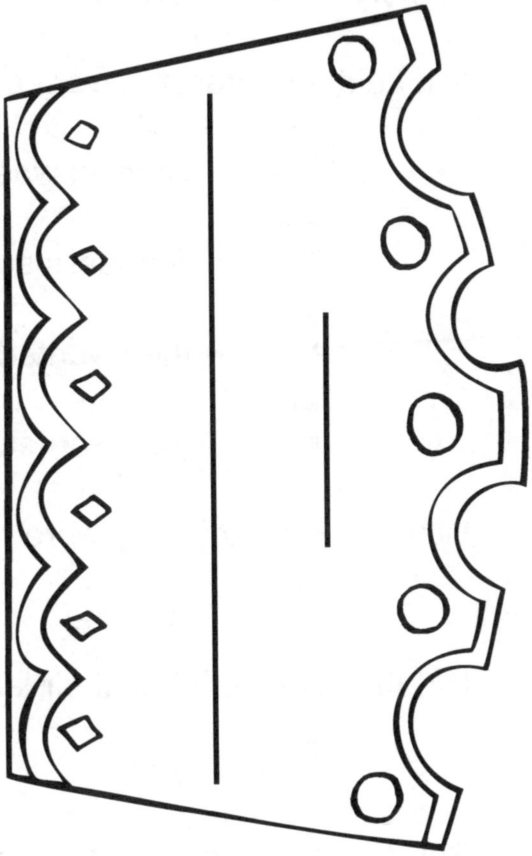

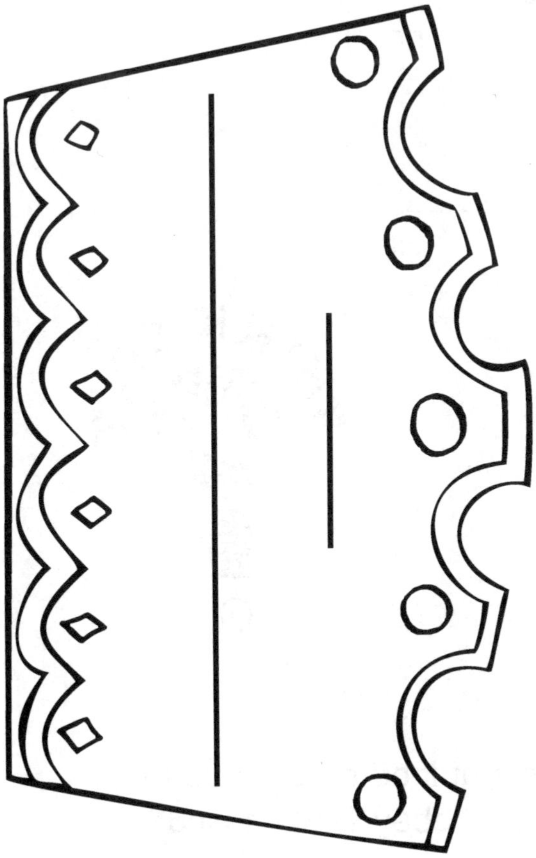

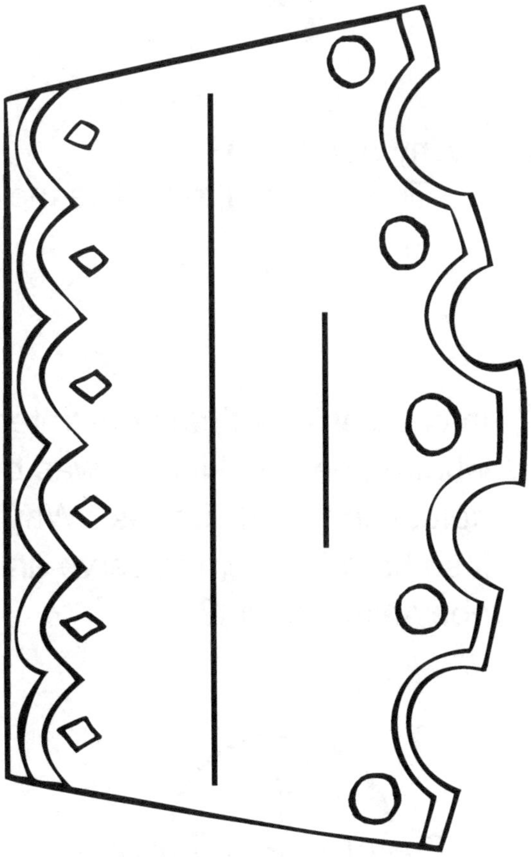

Today's story is from 1 Samuel 8:1 - 9:26.

1.   Why did the Israelites want a king (8:5)?

☐   Samuel was too old

☐   Samuel's sons were no good

☐   they wanted a change

☐   they wanted to be like everyone else

2.   Who did God say they were rejecting (8:7)?

☐   Samuel   ☐   God

3.   Did they want God as their king?

☐   yes   ☐   no

4.   Samuel told them about the things a king would do. Did they listen (8:19)?

☐   yes   ☐   no

5.   Why not (8:20)?
      They wanted to be like the other _ _ _ _ _ _ _ .

In chapter 7 God demonstrated what a powerful king he was by defeating the Philistines. Why was it so hard for them to serve and obey him as king?

THINK SPOT

Discussion Time

Why might it be hard for us to serve and obey God as king?

Do we ever want to be like everyone else?

WEEK 8
Made King

Preparation:
Read 1 Samuel 9:26 - 10:27, using the Bible study notes to help you.

Lesson Aim:
To see that God sometimes allows us to have our own way to teach us a lesson.

10:1 The anointing marked out a man set apart by God for kingly office.

10:2-8 We are not sure of the location of Rachel's tomb, but it could be Ramah. Saul went towards Ramah, and then on to Gibeah (his home town), then on to Gilgal. The Philistines were well entrenched there. Saul was the true successor of the Judges (Samuel, etc.) and was directed by the Spirit of God. He is given reassurance that God has chosen him by these various signs.

10:9 The signs are all fulfilled. The one chosen for specific mention - Saul's prophesying, together with his being given a new heart, - perhaps emphasises that Saul was to give the people not just military security but also spiritual direction (see Deuteronomy 17:14-20).

10:14-16 We do not know why he has this discussion with his uncle rather than his father. The kingship is still a secret, even from his family.

10:17-27 The nation as a whole enters the picture (Joshua 7:16). This was the way the Lord showed his choice to his people. Samuel was probably referring to the institution given through Moses as set out in Deuteronomy 17:14-20.

The people wanted to put their trust in a king rather than in God alone. He permitted them to have a king but the subsequent history of Israel's kingship was proof that such trust was entirely misplaced.

Lesson Plan

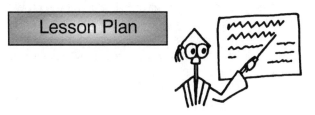

Start by asking the children how they would react if they were told they were king of the class for a day. Talk to them about whether they would be pleased to be chosen, what they would do about it, etc. Ask them if they can remember the name of the man who was chosen to be king in last week's lesson. In today's true story from the Bible we will find out how he reacted when he was made king. Tell the story.

At the end of the story go over Saul's reaction (10:20-24). Talk about God being his people's first king and what God had done for them (10:17-19). Were the people wise when they rejected God as their king? Revise the memory verse.

59

Visual Aids

Flannelgraph or pictures. You need Samuel, Saul, his servant and a crowd of people (see last week's lesson), a donkey, 3 goats, 3 loaves of bread, a wineskin, a group of prophets (see visual aids on pages 83-87).

When picking out the tribe have 1 person to represent each of the 12 tribes, then a number of people to represent the families, etc. It brings home to the children the drama of the choosing (see visual aids on pages 83-87).

Activities / 3 - 5s

Make a crown. Photocopy page 61 on card for each child. Prior to the lesson cut out the 2 halves of the crown, discarding the marked areas. Glue or sellotape the 2 halves together at one end. The children decorate their crowns with coloured stars, gummed paper shapes, silver foil, etc. Fit the crown on the child's head and staple or glue the 2 ends together to fit. Discuss with the children the fact that God is our king and that we show our love for him by obeying his word, the Bible.

Activities / 5 - 7s

Photocopy page 62 and the bottom of page 60 for each child. Prior to the lesson cut out the pieces of Saul from page 60 and place in an envelope for each child.

Instructions
- Assemble Saul by attaching A behind B and C behind B using split pin paper fasteners at the dots.
- Attach the legs to the rest of the figure by placing D behind C and attaching them to the dot on the picture with a split pin paper fastener.

- Fold Saul up to hide among the luggage (see diagram). Then stand him up to see how tall he was.

Activities / 7 - 9s

Photocopy page 63 on card and page 64 on paper for each child. Go through page 64 as a class activity. Make up the model of Saul. Cut out Saul and base along the thick black line. Sellotape the base together so that he can stand up. Cut out the 2 crowns. Glue the tabs together and put crown 1 on Saul's head. Stick crown 2 on Saul's chest with bluetak (see diagram).

Activity for 5-7s

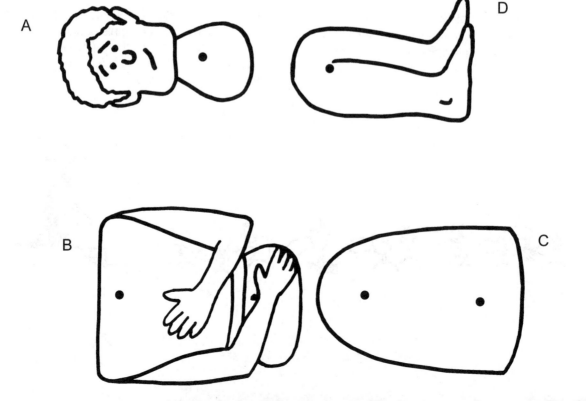

60

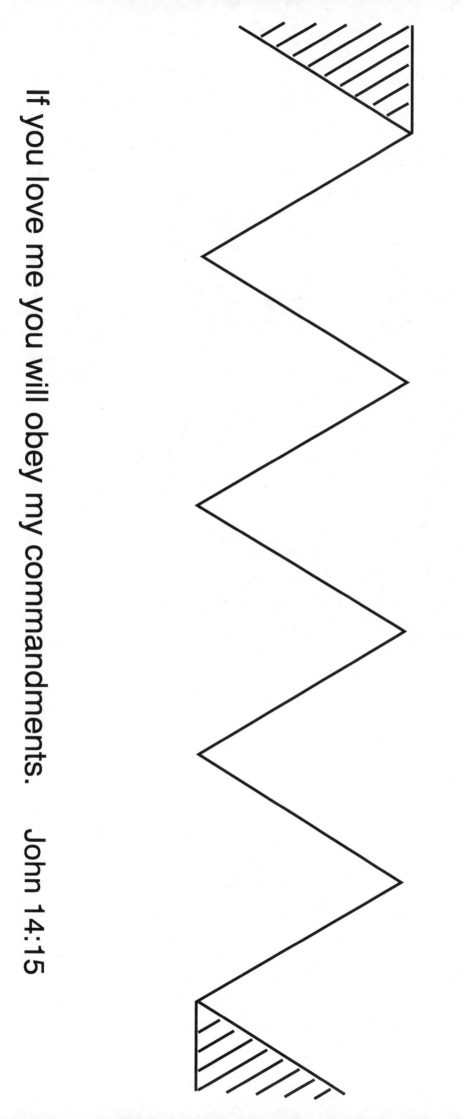

God is my king.

If you love me you will obey my commandments.   John 14:15

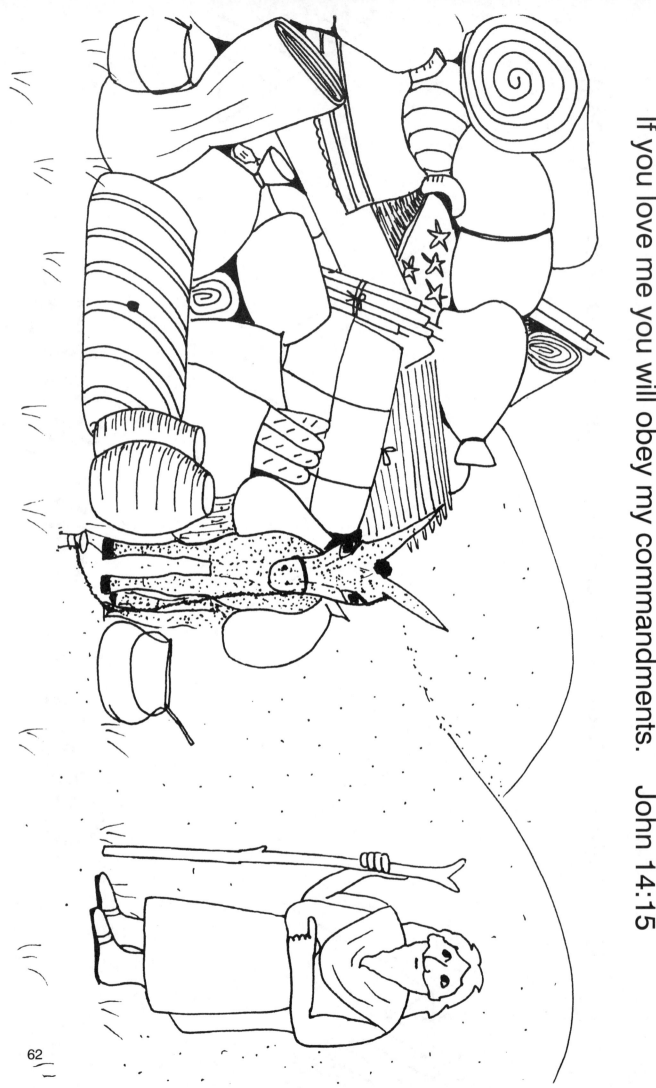

If you love me you will obey my commandments.   John 14:15

1

God
is my King
2

'How can this fellow save us?' (1 Samuel 10:27)
Did the Israelites learn this lesson?

Today's story is from 1 Samuel 9:26 - 10:27.

1.   Did Saul think he should be king (9:21)?

            ☐   yes   ☐   no

2.   Read 10:1-7 to see what signs Samuel gave Saul as a proof that God
        had anointed him king.

a)   At Zelzah Saul would meet ...... men, who would tell him that the
        _ _ _ _ _ _ _   had been found.

b)   At the great tree of Tabor Saul would meet ...... men carrying ......
        young goats, ... loaves of bread and ...... skin of wine. They would
        give Saul ...... loaves of bread.

c)   At Gibeah Saul would meet some prophets and would
        _ _ _ _ _ _ _ _   with them.

3.   Did those who knew Saul think he was the right person to be king
        (10:9-16)?

            ☐   yes   ☐   no

4.   In order to be a suitable king Saul would have to follow the
        regulations of kingship. Read Deuteronomy 17:14-20 to see what
        these were. If Saul was to lead his people who did he need to have
        as his king?

        ....

Discuss

Saul failed to follow the regulations
of kingship, as we shall see in the
next 2 lessons, so why did God
allow his people to have their own
way and have a human king?

Might God ever allow us to have our
own way to teach us a lesson?

Preparation:
Read 1 Samuel 13:1-16; 14:1-23, using the Bible study notes to help you.

Lesson Aim:
To teach the importance of obeying God.

13:5   Beth Aven is another name for Bethel.

13:8   Refer to 1 Samuel 10:8. The text there does not make it clear when he was to go to Gilgal but Samuel must obviously have discussed this with him. Only the gist of the conversation is given. Saul had already visited Gilgal before the events in chapter 13, according to chapter 11:14ff. It seems probable therefore, that Samuel was referring to the mustering there for battle, whenever that might take place.

13:8-9   We see Saul's impatience and lack of will to obey God in what he had been told.

13:11-13   Saul showed evidence of a relationship with God, and indeed the way he sought to appease God was almost superstitious. He was putting more trust in religious ceremony than in the word of God he had been given. Also, when confronted with his sin, rather than confessing and repenting of his error, he tried to defend himself. There is a vivid contrast here between Saul and David, who was prepared to confess his sins.

A further contrast comes out in the following chapter between Saul and his son Jonathan. Jonathan may have been impetuous and perhaps also thoughtless, but significantly, three times in the planning of his raid on the Philistines he refers to his awareness of the Lord's presence with him. He knew he could trust God. Saul did not, and the result of his disobedience was God's rejection of his dynasty.

Lesson Plan

Talk to the children about disobedience. Do they always do what they are told? Why do they disobey? What happens as a result? Are their parents happy when they disobey? Do they think God is happy when they disobey? Revise the memory verse. Remind the children of the previous 2 lessons using a question and answer format. In today's true story from the Bible we will see what Saul did when he was told to do something. Ask them to listen carefully so that they can tell you who gave Saul instructions and what he did about them. Concentrate on the story in 1 Samuel 13:1-16 for the younger children.

At the end of the story go over the questions. Point out to the children that when Saul was faced with his sin he did not say sorry, instead he made excuses.

Talk about the importance of saying sorry when we disobey, and really meaning it. Finish with a short time of prayer, encouraging the children to pray simple, one sentence, sorry prayers.

Visual Aids

Flannelgraph or pictures. You need Saul. Samuel, and an army. Use figures from the visual aids section on pages 83-87. Photocopy the crowd x 4 for Saul's army. Start with all the army on the board, then take 3 parts off to see the army decreasing in size.

Activities / 3 - 5s

Make a story box. Photocopy page 67 on paper and page 68 on card for each child. Prior to the lesson cut out the story box and make up as instructed on page 68. Cut out the pictures from page 67 and place in an envelope for each child. The children colour the pictures and glue them in order round the box. Use it to revise the story.

Activities / 5 - 7s

Make an identikit picture for Saul and one for Jonathan. Photocopy page 69 x 1 and page 70 x 2 for each child. Prior to the lesson cut out the pieces from page 69 and place in an envelope for each child. The children glue the appropriate pieces onto the 2 picture frames to make their identikit pictures. Glue the appropriate name and comments underneath each picture.

Activities / 7 - 9s

Photocopy the appropriate coded words back to back with page 74 for each child. (Page 71 is for use with NIV, page 72 with GNB and page 73 with KJV.) The test is to decode the words and write them in the sentences below. Knowing they have got it right comes from checking it against God's word. The answers to the questions on page 74 come from discussion of the 2 verses under the decoded words and the 1 Samuel passage. Do make sure the children realise the importance of knowing God's word and obeying it.

Disobeys God	Activity for 3-5s

The Philistine army was very big. The Israelites were afraid.

Samuel was late coming.

Saul disobeyed God. He offered the sacrifice.

Samuel told Saul God was angry. God would choose another king.

Story Block
Cut out, score and fold along
dotted lines. Glue the 4th side
to the other 2 sides. Glue the
top flaps inside the sides to
make a box open at the
Bottom.

side

God tests Saul
1 Samuel 13:1-16; 14:1-23

If you love me you will obey
my commandments.
John 14:15

top

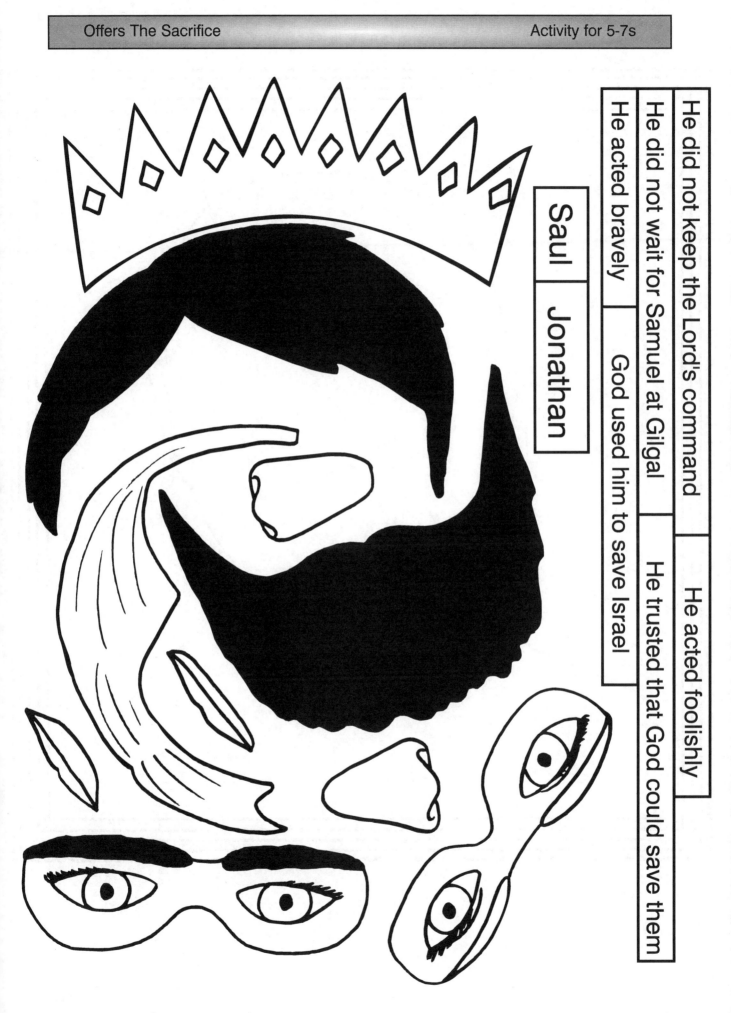

Saul | Jonathan

He did not keep the Lord's command

He did not wait for Samuel at Gilgal

He acted bravely

God used him to save Israel

He acted foolishly

He trusted that God could save them

Use the code to discover the following words.

a	b	c	d	e	f	g	h	i	j	k	l	m

NIV

n	o	p	q	r	s	t	u	v	w	x	y	z

Now, using the words, fill in the gaps in the 2 verses below. When you have finished, look up the verses to check if you are correct.

Consider it pure .... , my brothers, whenever you face ....
of many kinds, because you know that the .... of your
.... develops ....
James 1:2-3

No .... has seized you except what is common to man. And
.... is faithful; he will not let you be tempted beyond what you
can bear. But when you are tempted, he will also .... a way
out so that you can .... up under it. 1 Corinthians 10:13

Use the code to discover the following words.

✎	⬤	▶	🚂	🛋	🧸	🚪	🧑‍🤝‍🧑	🚿	▱	⛴	🚋	◎
a	b	c	d	e	f	g	h	i	j	k	l	m

🎁	🐟	🌧	☁	🌨	☁	☀	☁	🌞	💼	⚽	✏	🚲
n	o	p	q	r	s	t	u	v	w	x	y	z

GNB

Now, using the words, fill in the gaps in the 2 verses below. When you have finished, look up the verses to check if you are correct.

My brothers, ... yourselves fortunate when all kinds of .... come your way, for you know that when your .... succeeds in facing such trials, the result is the ability to ....
James 1:2-3

Every .... that you have experienced is the kind that normally comes to people. But .... keeps his .... , and he will not allow you be tested beyond your power to remain .... ; at the time you are put to the test, he will give you the .... to endure it, and so .... you with a way out.   1 Corinthians 10:13

Use the code to discover the following words.

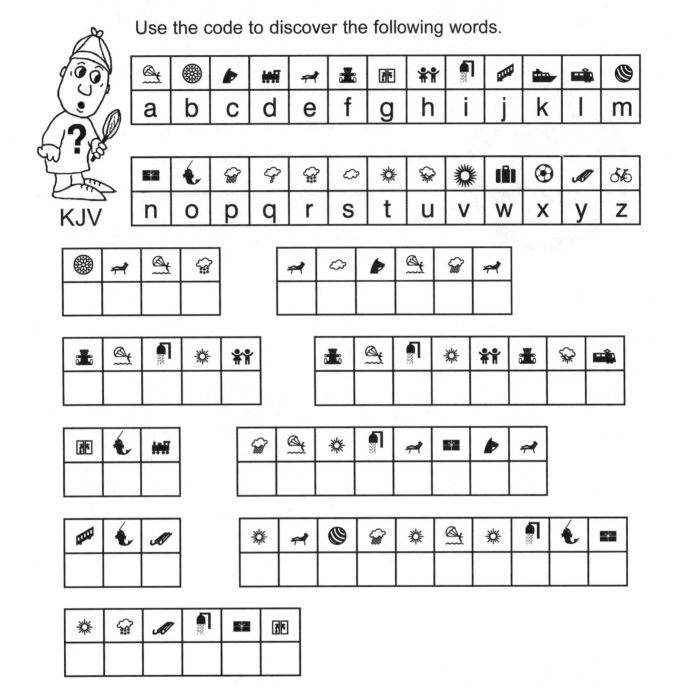

KJV

Now, using the words, fill in the gaps in the 2 verses below. When you have finished, look up the verses to check if you are correct.

My brethren, count it all .... when ye fall into divers temptations; knowing this, that the .... of your .... worketh ....
                                                                                James 1:2-3

There hath no .... taken you but such is common to man: but .... is .... , who will not suffer you be tempted above that ye are able; but will with the temptation also make a way to .... , that ye may be able to .... it.   1 Corinthians 10:13

Being tested is never pleasant.

Why does God allow us to be tested?

How did God test Saul?

Read 1 Samuel 13:5-13 to
see what happened when God
tested Saul. How did Saul fail
the test? Why?

How can we make sure that
when we are tested we will
not fail?

Thank God that he keeps his
promises. Ask him to help
you resist temptation.

Preparation:
Read 1 Samuel 15:1-35, using the Bible study notes to help you.

Lesson Aim:
To understand the result of repeated disobedience.

5:1　　This was a command from God.

15:2　　The Amalekites were the ancient enemy of Israel (Exodus 17:8-16) and were under divine judgment. For the older children give some thought to the question, 'Why should they kill the women and children?' One point to remember is that the people were seen as a collective unit; there was little stress on the individual. Because God's command was not carried out Israel was attacked for a further generation. God does not forget sin. It is punished.

15:4　　Telaim was in the Negeb, possibly a few miles south of Beersheba.

15:5　　The Kenites were always well disposed to Israel (Numbers 19:29-32, Judges 1:16).

15:11　　God feels sorrow that he made Saul king.

15:12　　Carmel is a place in south Judah.

15:23　　In 1 Samuel 13:13 Saul had been denied a dynasty. Now he is denounced in favour of another.

15:24　　Saul wants to put the blame elsewhere but the responsibility is his. He repeatedly disobeyed God, and as a consequence was rejected as king.

NB Do ensure that the children do not think that their repeated disobedience will mean rejection by their parents or by God; God has promised to forgive anyone who truly repents (1 John, 1:9). But do make sure that they understand that Saul's repeated disobedience and unwillingness to repent caused God to reject him as king. The older children need to understand that repeated disobedience causes the person to become hardened to that particular sin and leads to an unwillingness to admit he/she is wrong.

Lesson Plan

Start with a simple quiz to see what the children have remembered from the previous 3 weeks. Divide the children into 2 teams. Each team requires a large crown cut from coloured card or paper and 6 diamond shapes to be jewels. In advance prepare 12-14 questions on the previous 3 lessons. Pin up the crowns on a board. The teams take it in turns to answer a question. When a right answer is given a jewel is added to their crown. The first team to get all 6 jewels on their crown is the winner. If both teams achieve this in the same round a draw is declared. Use the end of the quiz to lead into today's story.

At the end of the story go over Saul's reaction when faced with his sin - making excuses and blaming other people. Point out that we all tend to do the same when we are found out in wrongdoing. Do ensure that the children know that God has promised to forgive us if we are truly sorry for wrongdoing (1 John 1:9). Revise the memory verse.

Visual Aids

Flannelgraph or pictures. You need Samuel and Saul from the visual aids section on pages 83-87 and the animals from page 66.

Activities / 3 - 5s

Photocopy the bottom of page 66 and page 77 for each child. Prior to the lesson cut out the animals from page 66 and place in an envelope for each child. The children colour the picture. Ask them how Samuel knew Saul had disobeyed God - what he heard when he came to Saul's camp. Get the children to make the animal noises. Glue the animals onto the picture and either colour them or glue on scraps of furry material.

Activities / 5 - 7s

Photocopy page 78 on paper and page 79 on card for each child.

Instructions
- Cut out the pieces of the pyramid and the pictures.
- Colour the pictures and glue them onto the appropriate parts of the pyramid.
- Score and fold the pieces of the pyramid along the dotted lines. Glue the 2 separate triangles to the main part of the pyramid, being careful to glue triangle A to flap A and triangle B to flap B with the words at the base of the triangle. Glue the tabs to the inside. Make up the pyramid by gluing the 4 side flaps to the inside. The story can be read clockwise around the pyramid with the result of Saul's actions on the base.

Activities / 7 - 9s

A revision game. Photocopy page 80 enlarging to A3 size and glue onto card to make a game board. Photocopy pages 81 and 82 onto card and cut out to make a pack of question cards. Follow the instructions on page 80. The game is suitable for a maximum of 6 players, so either provide one game for every 5/6 children or get the children to play in pairs.

The game is to revise the Saul series and to teach that sinning has consequences. Each snake represents temptation. A correct answer (i.e. knowing God's word) avoids temptation. An incorrect answer means going backwards in the game and thus incurring a penalty. At the end point out that although some snakes seem initially to be a short cut (6 and 24), they always end further back.

Make sure that the children are aware that going to heaven is not a result of amassing Brownie points for avoiding temptation, but on what Jesus has done for those who believe in him.

Saul disobeyed God; he kept all the best animals. So God rejected Saul as king.

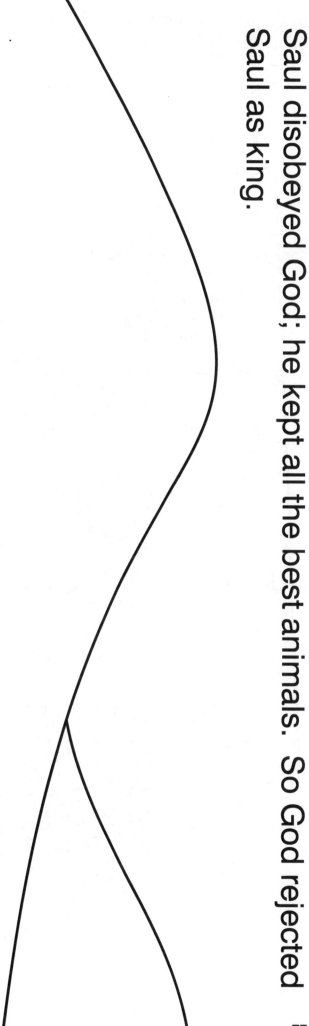

Jesus said, "If you love me you will obey my commandments.'
John 14:15

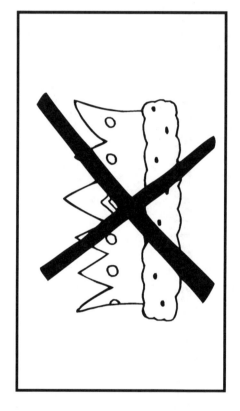

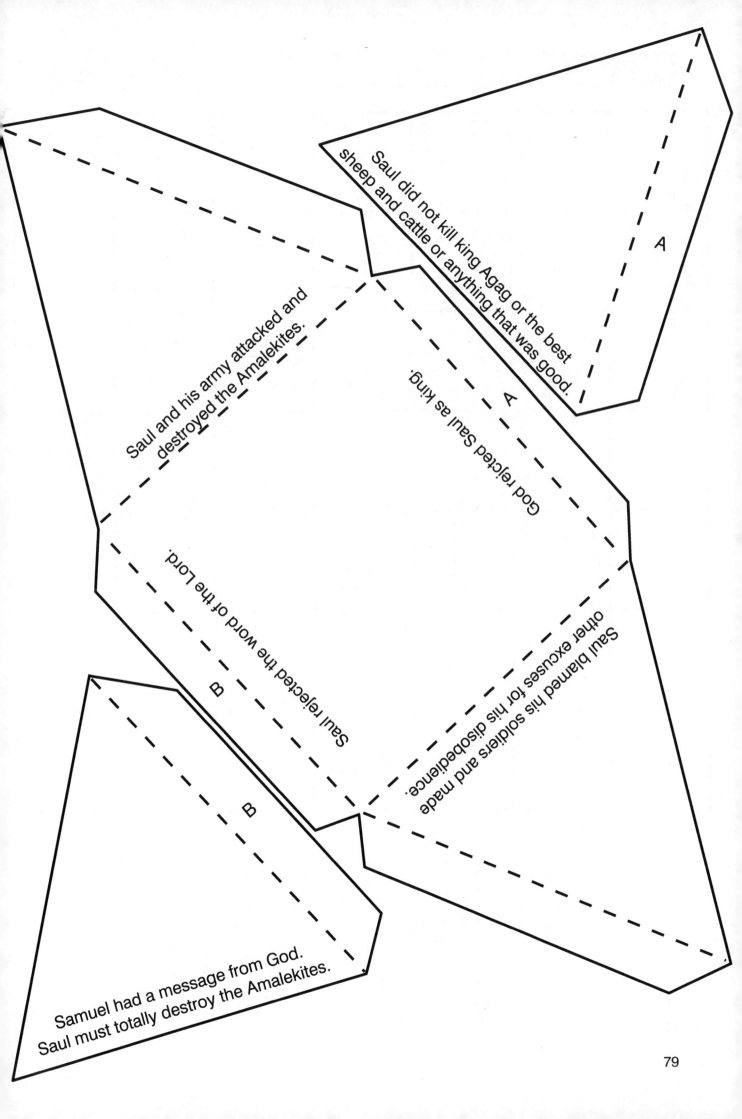

Saul did not kill king Agag or the best sheep and cattle or anything that was good.

A

A

God rejected Saul as king.

Saul and his army attacked and destroyed the Amalekites.

Saul blamed his soldiers and made other excuses for his disobedience.

Saul rejected the word of the Lord.

B

B

Samuel had a message from God. Saul must totally destroy the Amalekites.

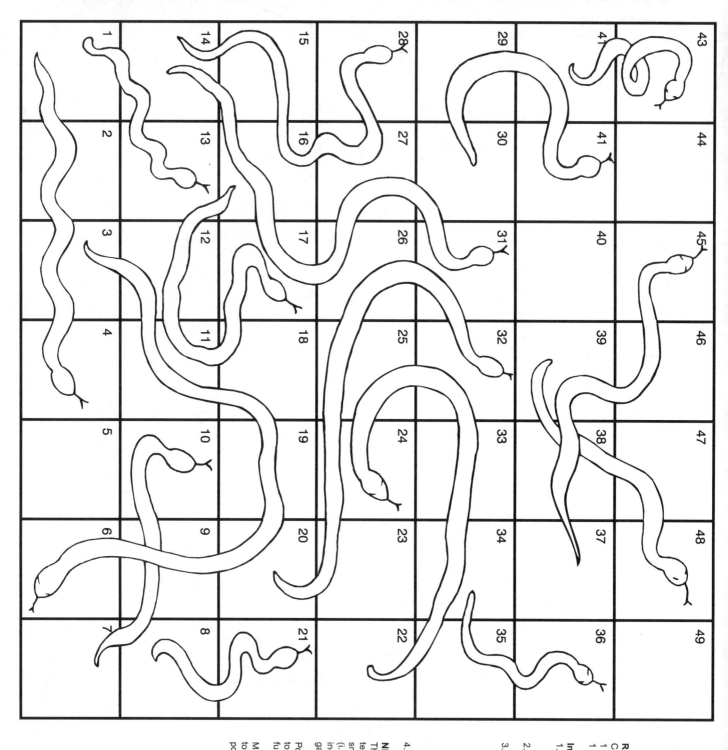

Required
Counters for each player.
1 dice
1 pack of Question cards (shuffled).

Instructions
1. Throw the dice to decide who starts - the person who throws the highest number.

2. The play then moves in a clockwise direction.

3. Each player throws the dice and moves the number thrown. If he/she lands on the head of a snake, one of the other players takes the top card off the question pile and asks the question. If the question is answered correctly the player is safe and remains on that square. An incorrect answer means that the player slides down to the tail of the snake.

4. The first player to reach square 49, wins.

NB for the teacher
This game is for revision of the Saul series and to teach that sinning has consequences. Each snake represents temptation. A correct answer (i.e. knowing God's word) avoids temptation. An incorrect answer means going backwards in the game and thus incurring a penalty.

Point out that although some snakes initially seem to be a short cut (6 and 24), they always end further back.

Make sure that the children are aware that going to heaven is not a result of amassing Brownie points for avoiding temptation!

Q	What does John 14:15 say?	Q	What does John 14:15 say?	Q	What does John 14:15 say?
A	If you love me you will obey my commands.	A	If you love me you will obey my commands.	A	If you love me you will obey my commands.
Q	Where in the Bible is found 'If you love me you will obey my commands'?	Q	Where in the Bible is found 'If you love me you will obey my commands'?	Q	Where in the Bible is found 'If you love me you will obey my commands'?
A	John 14:15	A	John 14:15	A	John 14:15
Q	To whom did the people go to ask for a king?	Q	Why did the Israelites want a king?	Q	By asking for a king what were the Israelites doing to God?
A	Samuel	A	To be like the other countries/to lead them into battle.	A	Rejecting him as their king.
Q	What was the name of the first earthly king of Israel?	Q	Who chose the first king of Israel?	Q	What tribe did Saul come from?
A	Saul	A	God	A	Benjamin
Q	What was there about Saul that made him a good choice?	Q	What was Saul doing when he first met Samuel?	Q	What did God give to Saul after he was anointed as king?
A	He was tall and handsome (he looked like a king).	A	Looking for lost donkeys.	A	A new nature (1 Samuel 10:9)

Q Who were the Israelites fighting against when Saul offered the sacrifice at Gilgal?	**Q** Was the Philistine army at Gilgal bigger or smaller than the Israelite army?	**Q** Why did Saul offer the sacrifice at Gilgal?
A The Philistines	**A** Bigger	**A** Samuel was late arriving and the army was frightened.
Q What was wrong with Saul offering the sacrifice?	**Q** What was the name of Saul's son?	**Q** Why were Jonathan and his armour-bearer able to defeat the Philistines?
A He was not a priest (he came from the tribe of Benjamin).	**A** Johnathan	**A** Because God was helping them.
Q Why did God reject Saul as king?	**Q** What was the name of the king of Amalek?	**Q** What did God tell Saul to do to the Amalekites?
A Disobedience	**A** Agag	**A** Destroy everything - all the people and all the animals.
Q When the Israelites beat the Amalekites what did they do that was wrong?	**Q** Did Saul believe that what the Israelites did to the Amalekites was wrong?	**Q** What did Saul answer when Samuel told him he had disobeyed God's order about the Amalekites?
A They left king Agag alive, saved the best animals, only destroyed what was worthless.	**A** No	**A** My men did it. We kept the best to offer to God.
Q What does God think is better than sacrifices?		
A Obedience		

Visual Aids

Photocopy, enlarge and cut out as required.

Manoah

wife

hair

jawbone

angel

Photocopy, enlarge and cut out as required.

Philistine girl

Delilah

Samson (add hair from previous page)

Photocopy, enlarge and cut out as required.

Mahlon and Chilion

Elimilech

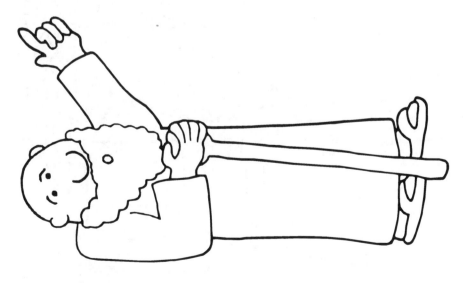

Samuel

Visual Aids

Photocopy, enlarge and cut out as required.

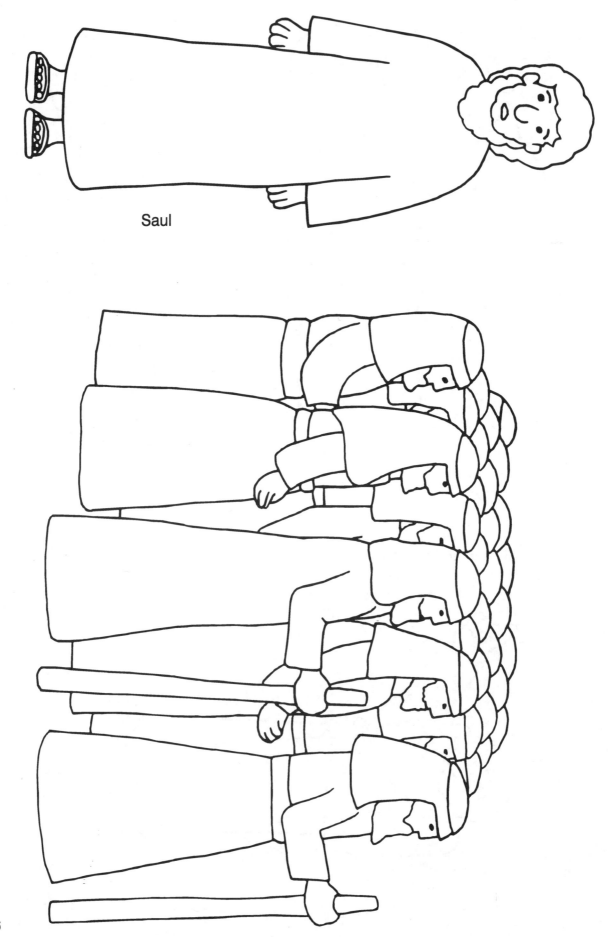

Saul

86

Photocopy, enlarge and cut out as required.

man - photocopy number required for choosing Saul

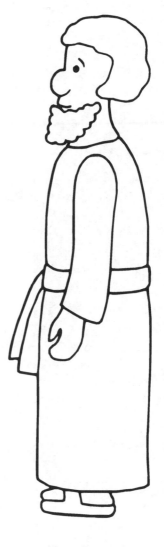

Saul's servant

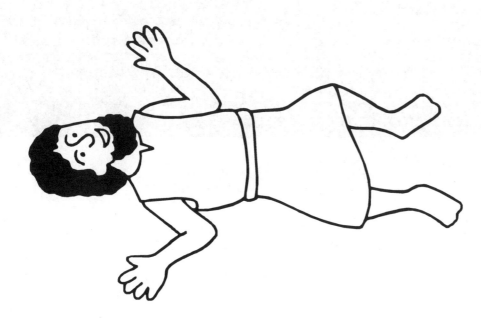

dancing prophet

wine skin and
loaves of bread

Syllabus for On The Way for 3-9s

	Year 1	Year 2	Year 3
	Book 1 (13 weeks)	**Book 6 (10 weeks)**	**Book 11 (13 weeks)**
Old/New Testament	In the Beginning (3) Abraham (6) Jacob (4)	Samson (2) Ruth (2) Samuel (2) Saul (4)	Jesus Meets (3) God's Rules (10)
	Book 2 (12 weeks)	**Book 7 (13 weeks)**	**Book 12 (14 weeks)**
Christmas *New Testament*	Christmas gifts (5) Jesus' Authority (7)	The Christmas Story (4) Preparation for Service (4) The Promised Messiah (5)	Heavenly Messengers (5) Jesus Helps (5) Parables of the Kingdom (4)
	Book 3 (13 weeks)	**Book 8 (9 weeks)**	**Book 13 (13 weeks)**
New Testament *Easter* *Early Church*	Prayer (4) Jesus is King (5) Peter (4)	Jesus Teaches (5) Parables of Judgment (2) The Easter Story (2)	Parables of the Vineyard (3) Jesus our Redeemer (3) The Early Church (3) Paul (4)
	Book 4 (10 weeks)	**Book 9 (10 weeks)**	**Book 14 (14 weeks)**
Old Testament	Joseph (4) Job (1) Moses (5)	David (7) Solomon (3)	Kings (5) Daniel (4) Esther (2) Nehemiah (3)
	Book 5 (10 weeks)	**Book 10 (11 weeks)**	
Old Testament	In the Wilderness (4) Joshua (4) Gideon (2)	Elijah (5) Elisha (4) Jonah (2)	

The books can be used in any order; the above plan is the suggested order.
The syllabus is chronological; Christmas to Easter is all about Jesus, followed by 3 series on the early church (1 in Book 3 and 2 in Book 13). The rest of each year consists of lessons from the Old Testament. Old Testament and New Testament lessons are in separate books (apart from Book 11), so the books can be used in whatever order is required. The books contain differing numbers of lessons, so that they fit the required number of weeks between Christmas and Easter and the following Christmas.
The number in brackets indicates the number of lessons in a series.

For more information about *On The Way for 3-9s* please contact:
Christian Focus Publications, Geanies House, Fearn, Tain, Ross shire, IV20 1TW / Tel: (01862) 871 011 or
TnT Ministries, 29 Buxton Gardens, Acton, London, W3 9LE / Tel: +44(0)181 992 0450

Teacher's Challenge Solution

pages
7, 14,
27, 53,
65